NOISE THINKS THE ANTHROPOCENE

BEFORE YOU START TO READ THIS BOOK, take this moment to think about making a donation to punctum books, an independent non-profit press,

@ https://punctumbooks.com/support/

If you're reading the e-book, you can click on the image below to go directly to our donations site. Any amount, no matter the size, is appreciated and will help us to keep our ship of fools afloat. Contributions from dedicated readers will also help us to keep our commons open and to cultivate new work that can't find a welcoming port elsewhere. Our adventure is not possible without your support.

Vive la Open Access.

Fig. 1. Hieronymus Bosch, *Ship of Fools* (1490–1500)

First published in 2019 by dead letter office, BABEL Working Group
an imprint of punctum books, Earth, Milky Way.
https://punctumbooks.com

The BABEL Working Group is a collective and desiring-assemblage of scholar–gypsies with no leaders or followers, no top and no bottom, and only a middle. BABEL roams and stalks the ruins of the post-historical university as a multiplicity, a pack, looking for other roaming packs with which to cohabit and build temporary shelters for intellectual vagabonds. We also take in strays.

ISBN-13: 978-1-950192-05-2 (print)
ISBN-13: 978-1-950192-06-9 (ePDF)

LCCN: 2018968576
Library of Congress Cataloging Data is available from the Library of Congress

Book design: Vincent W.J. van Gerven Oei

HIC SVNT MONSTRA

NOISE THINKS THE ANTHROPO-CENE

AN EXPERIMENT IN NOISE POETICS

AARON ZWINTSCHER

(P)

To Finnegan,
my eager listener

CONTENTS

INTRODUCTION——————————————————————15

METHODS I: DEVELOPING THORYBOLOGY——————————41
METHODS II: THINKING THE ANTHROPOCENE————————49
TOWARDS A POSSIBLE NOISE POLITICS——————————55
HOSPITALITY————————————————————————65
~~NOISE~~——————————————————————————73
BEING-AS-NOISE————————————————————79
REINHABITING THE EARTH—————————————————85
NOISE, ECOLOGY, AND THE QUESTION OF NATURE——————91
CONCERNING SILENCE ————————————————————95
REPETITION/BLURRING BOUNDARIES——————————————99
NEITHER MEANING NOR FINALITY—————————————103
REPETITION/ZONES OF INDETERMINACY——————————107
THE WANDERING PATH————————————————————111
IN THE FACE OF HORROR——————————————————115
INTERPRETING ~~NOISE~~———————————————————119
CLARITY————————————————————————————123
INDETERMINATE CONCLUSIONS——————————————127

AFTERWORD: A REASSESSMENT————————————————131

LIST OF REFERENCES———————————————————137

ACKNOWLEDGMENTS

At times, it feels as if this is the sort of project for which one asks forgiveness in addition to acknowledging all the assistance and encouragement I got along the way. So first, let me say to all of you who put up with it: sorry about all the noise.

Certainly I would like to acknowledge and thank my advisors in the Texts & Technology Ph.D. program. Barry Mauer introduced me to the theory and avant-garde textual practices of Gregory Ulmer and encouraged my pursuit of academic work in alternative grammars. Anthony Grajeda taught me about and got me intrigued in the possibilities of sound and noise, turning me on to Steve Goodman (which led on to so many other fringe and para-academic theoretical works). Angela Rounsaville let me get away with digressive and fragmentary writing practices, works that intentionally jumped around (from film, to music, to culture, to theory), never settling. Mark Schafer, my outside reader, wasn't scared off by the unfamiliarity of the content or the methodology and kept me focused on the normative and practical possibilities of this work and noise theory in general. The latitude and encouragement that they all provided was what made this work possible in the first place.

I would further like to thank the Texts & Technology Ph.D. program, the College of Arts and Humanities, and the University of Central Florida for being understanding and patient with me and for allowing, encouraging, and funding my research in wide-ranging and experimental directions.

I would like to acknowledge the conferences where I tested out these theories in various forms, most notably those of the Society for Literature and Science in the Arts. Through the papers that I presented and the feedback I received (as well as the numerous panels I attended and conversations I was able to have), I realized that while this work might be nonstandard, it was nowhere near so far beyond the pale as I had, at times, feared.

I would like to thank the theorists, writers, artists, philosophers, thinkers, and poets who have gone before and done similar things, blazing this trail, making such thoughts thinkable, and who generously and unknowingly offered up their words to be cut, scratched, and remixed into this experimental production.

I would like to thank my supportive family. My mother, who tirelessly read through multiple drafts of textual nonsense and then thanked me for offering her a chance to improve her vocabulary, was my guide for the flow of the work. By the end, she was unable to tell where I started and the quoted fragments left off, certain that even quotations sounded just like me. My son Finnegan never missed a chance to help me experience "noise," because he knows I love it even if he is not sure what it is. And my wife Gina, thank you most of all. You kept me focused, tethered, and on track throughout the entire process, you made sure the process kept moving forward, and you gave me the space and time to craft this cacophony.

I would like to thank everyone at punctum books who has worked making this experiment into a book. Particularly, I would like to thank Eileen Fradenburg Joy for her enthusiastic acceptance and support of the project and my editor, Vincent W.J. van Gerven Oei, for actually knowing Greek.

INTRODUCTION

Disclaimer How do I introduce this work, this textual assemblage infected with audiovisual distractions, this machine abandoned to run down in a barren desert? Perhaps it is best if I begin with a disavowal: this is not mine, I did not write it, this is a work and performance of noise/art/theory. That is melodramatic but not far off the point. This text is, in simplest terms, an assemblage of quotations from theory, fiction, poetry, criticism, and other disparate noise works that I had, after sprawling and digressive reading and research, ready to hand, cut up and remixed with my own arguments on noise and my own audiovisual noise art. I thus did not write it, but rather wrote with it, improvised over its changes.[1] It exists as an

---

1   The majority of this text is built and adapted from quotations. The quotations in the main body of the text are quoted in an inconsistent and fragmentary manner as many have been written over or modified to suit the needs of this text rather than their original context. The multiple rewritings of the quoted and randomly assembled text led to a final product that is significantly distant from the original samples borrowed from the work of other writers. However, there is a danger that the experimental model and style of this text opens it to accusations of plagiarism. This is not the case. While the main text writes over and thorough quotations in order to develop its position, the quotes are fully accounted for in Appendix B and each cited source is faithfully listed in the List of References. While

effort to establish a noise theory and create a work of that noise theory that is itself noisy: a work that operates in the milieu it analyzes.

████ This project began with a noise, became an experiment, and resulted in a theoretical framework. The content of this project is noise, or more specifically, text(s) addressing the concept of noise. But the focus of the project, the goal of the work, is to address (and ideally alter) a concept even more broad: our being-in-the-world in the Anthropocene. With regard to our being-in-the-world or the many crises of the moment, noise is not the answer. In fact, noise may not even be *an* answer. Noise, rather, is a question, a questioning, a putting to the question. Noise is a means of interrogating systems and structures of meaning and power as and where they exist, to challenge and critique their seeming stability, their univocity. It is a means of disturbing the so-called natural, and calling into question the very idea of nature.

Fragments, Traces, Remains The project was a product of tracing. Of wandering through the garden of forking paths, taking turns as they developed.

████ In Information Theory, noise is understood as the background of a signal. This theory depends on binary oppositions—noise/signal, background/foreground, environment/object. Timothy Morton's work on environments and nature and their fraught relationships to ecology came into play here. The notion that environments and nature are passive backgrounds upon which the drama of human culture and existence plays out is pervasive. Nature is located "over there," in some pristine beyond untouched and unspoiled by human

████

this text does not use a standard model of citation as it builds its argument from the work of others, in no way does it contend that it is not a work built from the work of others. There are many precedents for writing and citing in a similar manner, including but not limited to Walter Benjamin's *The Arcades Project*, Mark Amerika's *remixthebook*, the writings of Kathy Acker, and significant portions of William Burroughs's cutups.

involvement, a notion that when expressed plainly, seems increasingly absurd and impossible. There is no beyond, there is nothing on this planet that is untouched by human involvement (that is the essence of the Anthropocene), and backgrounds and nature are not passive. What, after all, is nature? Is it the nonhuman animals? Because they are hardly passive, even if they intrude only weakly into the political concerns of the average human. Is it the plants and trees? For though they are predominantly immobile, they are hardly inactive, however they may seem to be on human timescales. Even the rocks and mountains and oceans are, on their own scales (temporal, atomic, etc.), dynamic and significant actors. (This is the essence of both Bruno Latour's Actor–Network Theory as well as the Object-Oriented Ontology of Morton, Graham Harman, Levi Bryant, Ian Bogost, and others.) Noise thus presented itself to me as a means of considering and thinking the interactions of binary opposites, including those relating to nature and ecology.

In following this thread, I worked my way through Michel Serres's concept of the parasite.[2] Serres's concept takes noise and articulates it as both the background term in the binary as well as an intruding third term that destabilizes the binary. One could additionally consider noise as the porous demarcation between binary oppositions, an articulation of the opposition that actively acknowledges that the division is impure, incomplete, and unstable. *The Parasite* also raised the question of hospitality toward noise. Combined with Jacques Derrida's reading of hospitality as an unconditional openness to the *arrivant* (a concept that Morton adapts as the strange stranger and reads in relation to ecology and ecological thinking and relationships), this approach opens up a possible ethics of noise and understanding of noise in ethics and its relations to the unknowable Other.

[2] Michel Serres, *The Parasite,* trans. Lawrence R. Schehr (Minneapolis: University of Minnesota Press, 2007).

█████ Noise in relation to hospitality also opens the path to its opposite: noise as a means of control and domination. Here we could follow the paths of sonic weapons like the Long Range Acoustic Device (LRAD), a sonic cannon that can be mounted on a ship, a truck, or aircraft, and which is used most often for crowd control. Indeed, the mere presence of one with the New York Police Department (NYPD) at the Occupy Wall Street protests (where the gathering protestors were forbidden from using any means of amplification whatsoever and thus revived traditional organizing tactics such as the People's Mic), set the tone for how the City understood the encampment; sound and noise and the power to wield them was deemed the sole purview of the State. I also traced the path of sonic torture, of the use of sound (often hard rock or metal music) played at high volume or silence (as a form of sensory deprivation), as a means for breaking down detainees held by the United States.[3] There is also the long history of noise abatement, a complex political strategy that in theory is laudable and in practice is often only a protection for the wealthy and connected, a shunting of the problem unto the disenfranchised (we might note specifically here airports and other transportation noise—a significant source) and those who cannot afford to move away from nearby neighborhoods or take on less auditorily damaging careers.

█████ Other paths opened and closed. Drones are heavily represented in noise music, drones here meaning long, sustained tones. But this term led conductively to drone workers and the drudgery of work in desperate need of revitalization, drone bees and the threat of colony collapse disorder (a product of the Anthropocene and indirect human interaction), and drone warfare and its complex politics and issues of control, command, and exploitation (not to mention its ties to the LRAD and thus another entry point to thinking about noise).

█████

3 Juliette Volcler, *Extremely Loud: Sound as a Weapon,* trans. Carol Volk (New York: The New Press, 2013).

Most drone pilots are based in the desert, many in a base just outside of Las Vegas, itself a city of contradictions. Nearby are the Nevada Test Site and Yucca Mountain (the location of the majority of nuclear tests and nuclear waste storage), further extending the questions of control and contamination, of noise as waste and pollution as well as power and dominance. These issues are further explored in Serres's *Malfeasance*.[4] Indeed, the wide-ranging work of Michel Serres, his writings on noise, knowledge, pollution, waste, ecology, the senses, and the relationship between the sciences and the humanities, might be considered the connective tissue that draws together all the disparate threads of thought that went into this project into a single tapestry, which, when seen from the back looks like a meaningless jumble.

█████ Deserts also draw us into the work of Gilles Deleuze and Félix Guattari, as the concept of the desert is central to their theorizing territorialization, deterritorialization, and reterritorialization. This concept of the desert de/reterritorialization is related to noise specifically in regard to the relationship that noise has with knowledge and signals: a relationship of continual flux and motion, as the bleeding edge of noise (especially in relation to music) continues to move further and further as new sonic regions are mapped out, marked as noise, only to be brought back into the Culture Industry as acceptably marketable sounds. And here we can see the connection to Theodor Adorno (including his thoughts on music, the negative, and aesthetics) and to Walter Benjamin (including his thoughts on technology, reproduction, and history). We can also see to relations here with the abject in Julia Kristeva and Georges Bataille and heresy in François Laruelle, drawing us back into questions of violence, excess, waste, and power.

█████ Each of these and more could be considered entry points, beginnings on a path through the twisting theories of

4   Michel Serres, *Malfeasance: Appropriation through Pollution?*, trans. Anne-Marie Feenberg-Dibon (Stanford: Stanford University Press, 2010).

noise and the shape-shifting role of noise within philosophy and theory. Noise delineates and escapes every cage it is placed in. (John Cage plays no small role in this text and is afforded a mention in nearly every text that even tangentially links to noise.) And this does not yet fully include the paths and concepts exploited in the creation and navigation (Serres routinely relates noise to nausea—a potential though uncertain etymology—and to seafaring and navigation) of these concepts within the text itself. The noise and silence work of Cage connected to his indeterminacy and his Zen. His methods related to those of *musique concrète,* which connected to the cutups of William Burroughs, which linked to the collages of Dada and Surrealism, which linked to the noise of Merzbow (Masami Akita), which linked to the art and collage of waste and excess of Kurt Schwitters, which linked to the remix theory of Mark Amerika, and so on. Paths led on to paths, to dead ends, to crossings and recrossings, in a labyrinth, or again, alluding to Borges, a garden of forking paths. Some paths expanded, some paths narrowed. Some concepts remain only in the raw text data and would only be recognized obliquely. As the paths wandered and as I wandered the paths, I developed a total but non-totalizing philosophy of noise, a means of hearing and understanding noise and the noise inherent in the system, in our being-in-the-world. This is the noise I would like to introduce you to in the pages to come.

Demarcating Noise; or, Noise Is Everywhere and In Everything   Primarily, works of noise research set out to understand noise under (often) unacknowledged constraints drawn from mainstream academic discourse. Paul Hegarty's work is primarily based on musicology. Douglas Kahn's is primarily based in modern art criticism, including but not limited to music. Hillel Schwartz's work takes a historical approach. Bart Kosko addresses noise from the perspective of science and technology. Greg Hainge's work is the closest to mine as it seeks the philosophical—specifically, the ontological—underpinnings of noise, but he does not do so experimentally. These works, as well as much of the expanding fields of noise and sound studies, begin with the provisional definition of noise as it is used within their texts (in relation to music, in relation to sound, in relation to silence, in relation to technology, in relation to vibration, in relation to war) and the authors and theorists set those definitions, implicitly or explicitly, against other possible articulations of noise that they will not address.

This issue of definitions and conceptual clarity creates an issue for any sustained study of noise. As Hegarty puts it in his book: "What exactly noise is, or what it should do, alters through history, and this means that any account of noise is a history of disruptions and disturbances."[5] As he phrases it in an article: "When we ask what noise is, we would do well to remember that no single definition can function timelessly—this may well be the case with many terms, but one of the arguments of this essay is that noise is that which always fails to come into definition."[6] Or as Hainge writes:

> For whilst noise may seem like an eminently unproblematic term, concept or phenomenon when one does not really attend to it—and, as claimed here, we spend most of our time attempting not to attend to it—as soon as one does stop to think about what noise actually is, one quickly realizes that its meanings and definitions are highly subjective and unstable.[7]

And Hainge continues: "Rather, noise is immersive because there is nothing outside of it and because it is in everything."[8] Kahn counters/contrasts: "We know [noises] are

---

5 Paul Hegarty, *Noise/Music: A History* (New York: Bloomsbury, 2007), ix.
6 Paul Hegarty, "Noise Threshold: Merzbow and the End of Natural Sound," *Organized Sound* 6, no. 3 (2001): 193–200, at 193.
7 Greg Hainge, *Noise Matters: Towards an Ontology of Noise* (New York: Bloomsbury, 2013), 5.
8 Ibid., 13.

noises in the first place because they exist where they shouldn't or they don't make sense when they should. But here too in knowing this we already know too much for noise to exist."[9] Garret Keizer notes:

> Noise also compels us to seek our understanding through different filters. I can think of few subjects that lend themselves so readily to a multidisciplinary approach. Physicists, musicians, historians, psychologists, artists, engineers, and philosophers have all lent their ears and their expertise to its challenges. Noise is a complex phenomenon that reveals our complexity as human beings.[10]

▮▮▮▮ Michel Serres extends the idea: "In the beginning is the noise; the noise never stops. It is our apperception of chaos, our apprehension of disorder, our only link to the scattered distribution of things."[11] This is but a brief sampling of mostly related quotations about the concept and study of noise. Quotations dealing with thermal noise or noise pollution use completely different metaphors. As Merzbow, the godfather of noise music, poetically phrases it: "Noise is the nomadic producer of differences."[12]

▮▮▮▮ Noise for musicology relates to unorganized sound. Noise for wider art criticism deals with disorganization as well as disruption. Noise art expands the definition of noise to include unorganized/underorganized sound as well as the disruptive art practices of movements like Fluxus. Noise for communication is both the opposite of a signal but also the possibility of change (and thus information) in a signal and the

▮▮▮

9 Douglas Khan, *Noise Water Meat: A History of Sound in the Arts* (Cambridge: MIT Press, 1999), 21.

10 Garret Keizer, *The Unwanted Sound of Everything We Want: A Book About Noise* (New York: PublicAffairs, 2010), 243.

11 Serres, *The Parasite*, 126.

12 Masami Akita, quoted in Brett Woodward, *Merzbook: The Plesuredome of Noise* (Melbourne: Extreme, 1999), 9.

channel by which a signal can travel from emitter to receiver. Noise within a historical analysis is again a broader term as it includes the sounds of people and cities (church bells, traffic from horse carts through to jet aircraft and boom cars, the din of the marketplace and the crowd), as well as the history of noise abatement campaigning.

████ Noise abatement campaigns have existed in varying formal and informal capacities since the formation of cities and the placement of people in close proximity. John Stewart articulates the issue plainly: "Noise, however, is the pollutant which disturbs more people in their daily lives than any other."[13] But what noise represents to those campaigns is a product of taste and preference such as one type of music over another, or the appropriate place to hear music, the acceptable times for traffic and commerce, the amount of allowable sound associated with that traffic and commerce, which often manifest unspoken and unaddressed class and ethnic tensions. Keizer offers further nuance: "Noise is a weak issue also because most of those it affects are perceived, and very often dismissed, as weak. The ones who dismiss them, in addition to being powerful, are often the ones making the noise."[14] Thus, he relates, "[n]oise forces us to ask knotty questions about what we want, what we don't want, and how we negotiate between the two."[15] And again:

> [W]hen we talk about noise today we are never far from issues that were already at the center of politics in Aristotle's time: issues such as the rights of citizens, the distribution of wealth, and the proper exercise of power. These remain useful avenues for understanding noise. No less important, noise can prove a useful avenue in understanding our political selves.[16]

████

13 John Stewart, *Why Noise Matters: A Worldwide Perspective on the Problems, Policies and Solutions* (New York: Earthscan, 2011), 1.
14 Keizer, *The Unwanted Sound of Everything We Want,* 4.
15 Ibid., 24.
16 Ibid., 47–48.

▮▮▮▮ Science further broadens the scope of noise, especially as it relates to concepts of thermal noise and heat. Kosko notes that because all objects give off heat (nothing exists at absolute zero), they all emit thermal noise. From his perspective, everything is, in that sense, noisy and thus the universe will both begin and end in noise.[17] The philosophical view draws these perspectives together, addresses and interweaves them. While I did not seek to articulate a specific ontology, as Hainge does in his work (I question the possibility of being able to articulate a single and unwavering definition or state of being for noise-as-such), I am following a similar philosophical approach. Unlike Hainge, my method seeks to be noisy and experimental, because, as I contend and demonstrate within this text, a noisy method is better positioned to address and utilize the interruptive impact and potential of noise that makes noise such a provocative topic of study. In putting noise to use rather than only describing noise (whether in general or specific terms), this text allowed chance, indeterminacy, and loss of control to affect composition, thus opening previously unexplored lines of thought with regard to the subject and applications of noise.

▮▮▮▮ Because of the nature of noise, there is no noise-as-such that is understandable or able to be apprehended by the human mind. While the concept of noise is articulated and understood at various levels and with various degrees of clarity, the fact of its (partial) understanding limits its noise, limits its ability to *be* noise so long as noise is understood as the absence of meaning, the absence of sense. The understood and understandable is signal, is meaning. So noise, even understood only in relation to the signal it is contrasted to, or simply as the shape of the unknown, ceases to be fully noise within human perception, becoming, not signal, but ~~noise~~.[18] Putting noise

▮▮▮

17 Bart Kosko, *Noise* (New York: Viking, 2006).
18 The concept of noise under erasure (~~noise~~), which is also extended to ~~silence~~, is elaborated further in the text in several sections. Primarily, though, it is used as a method of articulating a concept that by definition is meaningless and beyond the realm of sense in an academic argument.

under erasure, as ~~noise~~, is my attempt to approach the topic of noise with as much clarity as possible. In my argument, however, this means losing track of noise-as-such, so that one can better apprehend the articulable concept of noise. Even as an unknown unknown, we know too much about noise for it to lack meaning completely, for it to remain noise. This differs from the relational ontologies of noise that are proposed by Hainge and Hegarty. Notably, Hegarty believes that there cannot be noise without listening, that lacking a human subject to perceive and classify it, noise cannot be said to exist. I argue quite the opposite: once it has been perceived, it has been given meaning even if that meaning is only its being categorized under the term noise, within the bounds of the meaningless. Knowing that about noise, following Kahn, is "already knowing too much" for it to remain noise.

████   It is then as ~~noise~~ that we deal with this concept. It is against a noise that exists within a relationship to our perceptive faculties and is bound and defined and shaped and demarcated by our epistemological understandings that we contend. This includes questions of volume and decibels; that is, when something becomes "noise" because it is measurably too loud according to an agreed-upon level. Questions of location and time; that is, when something is called "noise" because it exists in a place or at a time that has been deemed unacceptable according to a standard. Questions of signal and meaning; that is, when something is deemed to be "noise" because it is not recognized as having meaning, as being an intentional signal according to convention. Questions of sound and music; that

████

Perhaps the distinction might be clarified with a reference to Taoism: "As for the Way, the Way that can be spoken of is not the constant Way; as for names, the name that can be named is not the constant name" (*Lao-Tzu: Te-Tao Ching,* trans. Robert G. Henricks [New York: Ballantine Books, 1989], 53). Thus, the noise that can be thought or spoken or named is not the constant noise. For clarity, then, I make an effort, once the concept of noise under erasure is introduced in the text, to make the distinction between the elusive concept of noise-as-such (rendered as "noise") and the articulable concept of noise (rendered as "~~noise~~").

is, when something is considered "noise" because it lacks the organization or presentation that would place it within the set categories of music or sound. As seen here, these categories of "noise" are not categories of ontology but of phenomenology, of perception and relation.

██████ Ontologically, noise is approached apophatically, understood in terms of its absence and lack in relation to the known and perceived, but only approached (as ~~noise~~) and never fully apprehended within thought or concept. As Derrida notes of writing in *Limited Inc,* we might understand as similar for noise-as-such (or as close as we can approximate and think the concept): "No context can entirely enclose it. Nor any code, the code here being both the possibility and impossibility of writing, of its essential iterability (repetition/alterity)."[19] There is no concept or perception of noise that is not noisy, that is not undercut by the noise that forbids the possibility of its assimilation into knowledge.

Constructing Thorybology: On Being-As-Noise My intention in this text has been to argue noise in a noisy manner, to make the experience of reading about noise be as much as possible an experience of reading noise. This method is drawn from John Cage. As he argues in relation to his own work: "My intention has been, often, to say what I had to say in a way that would exemplify it; that would, conceivably, permit the listener to experience what I had to say rather than just hear about it."[20] Thus, I have compiled here a noise work that is textually noisy and that is intercut with sonic and visual noise (see also the *bruit jouissance* project[21]). Perhaps, the desire to make a noisy

██████

19 Jacques Derrida, *Limited Inc,* trans. Samuel Weber and Jeffrey Mehlman (Evanston: Northwestern University Press, 1988), 9.

20 John Cage, *Silence,* 50th anniv. edn. (Middletown: Wesleyan University Press, 2011), xxix.

21 See below for a description of the *Ouvroir de Bruit Potentielle avec The New York Society for the Expression of Unnecessary Noise present "bruit jouissance" as performed by the Delta Brainwave Society* project.

noise work is not, at first, apparent or obvious. In making this work noisy, I am immediately alienating certain readers. In working with alternate and experimental methods, I cannot predict or guarantee my results in advance. Many might see that as an unnecessary risk. Works of noise studies have been published within established forms of knowledge production and dissemination, so why change that? Why risk needless confusion, alienation, and incomprehensibility? Because noise is confusion, alienation, and incomprehensibility, and the efficacy and value of noise lies in its confusion, alienation, and incomprehensibility. As the text indicates, seeing what noise can do means doing noise. Following Guy Debord, "[o]ur unfortunate times thus compel me, once again, to write in a new way."[22] Or, Gregory Ulmer: "The point to emphasize here is that the text that follows is an *experiment*: it is offered not as a proof or assertion of truth but as a trial or test."[23]

██████ Indeed, this work proceeds in line with how the Stefano Agosti describes Derrida's *Spurs* in his introduction to that text: The "thought refuses to proceed in a straight line, refuses to follow in the well-marked linear rut. No, it moves in directions that are multiple, multiplied and stratified."[24] Moreover, "[t]he writing says nothing, but only confuses and confounds. It forces what it says into the margins and then seizes upon these margins in such a way that nothing may settle there."[25] This is a consequence of the concept of noise, certainly, but it is also an intentional act, a means of understanding and playing with noise according to a model best suited to its indeterminate, undecidable nature (such as it can ever be pinned down to having a single nature/stable set of characteristics).

██

22 Guy Debord, *Comments on the Society of the Spectacle,* trans. Malcolm Imrie (New York: Verso, 2011), 2.

23 Gregory Ulmer, *Heuretics: The Logic of Invention* (Baltimore: Johns Hopkins University Press, 1994), 38.

24 Stefano Agosti, "Introduction" to Jacques Derrida, *Spurs: Nietzsche's Styles,* trans. Barbara Harlow (Chicago: University of Chicago Press, 1979), 21.

25 Ibid., 23.

"The interactions are dynamic and continuous, with feedback and feedforward loops connecting different levels with each other and cross-connecting machine processes with human responses."[26] In composing and improvising with the indeterminate changes of this text, I have thus also sought to develop the methodology and underlying philosophy of this text into what I hope can be expanded into a broader interdisciplinary field of study that I have called *thorybology*.[27]

██████ Because of the argument form, however, certain clarifications are in order. The work, while an assemblage of quotations, was edited, remixed, added to, and annotated to clarify theses on noise raised by the juxtapositions and lines of thought that were generated through the experiment. The published results are far less noisy than those produced by the initial experiment, though they do remain noisy. But without clarification, the project would have appealed, if at all, to a much narrower audience. This is not to say that the work is without contradiction. The argument of the text follows much of the methodology of a manifesto. The language employed is often certain and assertive, categorizing claims in terms of "always" or "never" even as those claims clash and dispute each other. While this formal certainty is not perfectly suited to a concept such as noise, a concept that is highlighted here for its uncertainty, indeterminacy, varied and contradictory definitions, and its inability to "always" be anything without simul-

██

26 N. Katherine Hayles, *How We Think: Digital Media and Contemporary Technologies* (Chicago: University of Chicago Press, 2012), 13.

27 I term my particular study of noise "thorybology" (from the Greek θόρυβος — noise). It is a broad-spectrum approach to noise as both object and metaphor that draws from numerous disciplines while not particularly claiming a disciplined stance of its own. While I have not included within this text all possible articulations of noise (the included uses from the hard sciences are not as numerous as those from the arts), thorybology is capable of sustaining the contradictions that such an inclusive strategy would entail. Thorybology is particularly geared towards the ontological question of being-as-noise and the implications raised by that question for reassessing the human role in the world in the Anthropocene both in relation to other humans as well as in relation to other beings and things.

taneously being something else, the contradiction is, in fact, one more of the many contradictions inherent in thinking and writing about noise. The Afterword serves to contextualize and clarify the noise experiment, its successes and failures, and its position within the greater conversation around the potentials of noise, including those mentioned above and especially as it relates to noise politics—a recurring focus of the text.

The Anthropocene and Thinking It This brings us to the question of the Anthropocene. A central conceit of this text is that there is value in positioning noise to "think the Anthropocene." This is not, perhaps, an intuitive, logical association and thus bears further explanation here. The Anthropocene is the proposed name for our current geological epoch, named to reflect the increasing human impact on the world to even the stratigraphic level. An effective definition of the Anthropocene is articulated by Elizabeth Kolbert in her Pulitzer Prize-winning *The Sixth Extinction: An Unnatural History*: "The word 'Anthropocene' is the invention of Paul Crutzen, a Dutch chemist who shared a Noble Prize for discovering the effects of ozone-depleting compounds."[28] Elizabeth Kolbert quotes Crutzen:

> "It seems appropriate to assign the term 'Anthropocene' to the present, in many ways human-dominated, geological epoch," [Crutzen] observed. Among the many geological-scale changes people have effected, Crutzen cited the following: ▮▮▮ Human activity has transformed between a third and a half of the land surface of the planet. ▮▮▮ Most of the world's major rivers have been dammed or diverted. ▮▮▮ Fertilizer plants produce more nitrogen than is fixed naturally by all terrestrial ecosystems. ▮▮▮ Fisheries remove more than a third of the primary production of the oceans' coastal waters. Humans

▮▮

28 Elizabeth Kolbert, *The Sixth Extinction: An Unnatural History* (New York: Picador, 2014), 107.

use more than half of the world's readily accessible fresh water runoff. ████ Most significantly, Crutzen said, people have altered the composition of the atmosphere.[29]

████ Further, "[c]ontinuing along this path for much longer, [scientists Kump and Ridgewell] continued, 'is likely to leave a legacy of the Anthropocene as one of the most notable, if not cataclysmic events in the history of our planet.'"[30] Eugene Thacker writes: "The world is increasingly unthinkable — a world of planetary disasters, emerging pandemics, tectonic shifts, strange weather, oil-drenched seascapes, and the furtive, always-looming threat of extinction."[31] In reaction to the climatic crises, Timothy Morton contends: "The ecological era we find ourselves in — whether we like it or not and whether we recognize it or not — makes necessary a searching revaluation of philosophy, politics, and art."[32] It is toward this searching revaluation of philosophy, politics, and art that this text and the thorybology it describes are geared towards thinking the Anthropocene.

████ Noise is, among other things, a concept of destabilized binaries and boundaries. "Noise is a turbulence, it is order and disorder at the same time, order revolving on itself through repetition and redundancy, disorder through chance occurrences, through the drawing of lots at the crossroads, and through the global meandering, unpredictable and crazy."[33] Ecology is, following the pioneering work of Morton, a question of destabilized binaries as well. He continually challenges, in his work, the seemingly stable boundaries of nature/culture, noise/silence, foreground/background, subject/environment.

████

29 Ibid., 108.

30 Ibid., 124.

31 Eugene Thacker, *In The Dust of This Planet: Horror of Philosophy, Vol. 1* (Hants: Zero Books, 2011), 1.

32 Timothy Morton, *Dark Ecology: For a Logic of Future Coexistence* (New York: Columbia University Press, 2016), 159.

33 Michel Serres, *Genesis,* trans. Geneviève James and James Nielson (Ann Arbor: University of Michigan Press, 1995), 59.

Noting specifically, "when you mention the environment, you
bring it into the foreground. In other words, it stops being the
environment."[34] Morton challenges the idea that nature is some
passive background against which human dominance plays
out, arguing instead that this is an error based on, among other
things, an unwillingness to focus on and individuate specific
objects within "nature," to focus on noises and backgrounds
and thus disrupt the seemingly neutral binary oppositions.
"[T]here is no such thing as an *environment*: wherever we look
for it we find all kinds of objects—biomes, ecosystems, hedges,
gutters and human flesh. In a similar sense, there is no such
thing as *Nature*."[35]

███ A further contention of the text that joins ecology, the
Anthropocene, and noise is the ontological concept I term "being-as-noise." Being-as-noise is a form of being-in-the-world
that I argue best defines humans during the Anthropocene and
potentially all human being-in-the-world. As Garret Keizer
puts it, "[n]oise is the fullest expression of what we are, the authentic voice of our age."[36] Serres makes the links between noise
and waste, pollution, and excess explicit: "Now everywhere
and all the time we hear sound waste, the rubbish and refuse
of engines, ventilators, air conditioning, waste disposal units,
reactors, grinders, tuners that saturate the old pugnacious
cesspit world of the owners."[37] The decibel levels that humans
produce and are able to produce overcome all except the most
extreme of natural sounds and those tend to be uncommon.
Yet if noise is conceptually extended to include waste, pollution, and excess, the being-as-noise of humanity— existing
in such a way as to disrupt rather than cohabitate—can be
understood as even more ontologically intrinsic to the spe-

34 Timothy Morton, *Ecology Without Nature: Rethinking Environmental
    Aesthetics* (Cambridge: Harvard University Press, 2007), 1.
35 Timothy Morton, *Realist Magic: Objects, Ontology, Causality* (Ann Arbor:
    Open Humanities Press, 2013), 42.
36 Keizer, *The Unwanted Sound of Everything We Want*, 241.
37 Serres, *Malfeasance: Appropriation Through Pollution?*, 54.

cies. In commenting on the megafauna extinction that can be linked to seemingly benign (within human timescales) hunting practices, Elizabeth Kolbert notes that "[t]hough it might be nice to imagine that there once was a time when man lived in harmony with nature, it's not clear that he ever really did."[38] She continues:

> Indeed, this capacity [to change the world] is probably indistinguishable from the qualities that made us human to begin with: our restlessness, our creativity, our ability to cooperate to solve problems and complete complicated tasks. As soon as humans started using signs and symbols to represent the natural world, they pushed beyond the limits of that world.[39]

Based on these arguments, this text makes the claim that being-as-noise (a form of existence defined by its disruptive capacity) is likely inherent in the human species. It contends, though, that this capacity, when confronted directly (by thinking noise, by thinking ecology, by thinking climate change and the Anthropocene) can be directed away from destructive ends and towards creative coexistence.

A Note on Methodology   The development of the experimental methodology for this textual project began while I was working on the University of Central Florida Texts & Technology Dissertation Research Grant-funded *Ouvroir de Bruit Potentielle avec The New York Society for the Expression of Unnecessary Noise present "bruit jouissance" as performed by the Delta Brainwave Society*[40] project. That work is primarily composed of

---

38 Kolbert, *The Sixth Extinction*, 235.

39 Ibid., 266.

40 The *bruit jouissance* project functions as audio/visual supplement/ soundtrack to the present text. The concepts presented here are also present within the noise/music and visual noise of the project, though present differently because of the natures of the different media and the different

assembled and remixed fragments of sound (often field record-
ings) that have been cut together and juxtaposed for effect and
then processed into a completed form. The form that the *bruit
jouissance* project was taking, combined with the confluence
of theories that I had been applying in my noise research — the
indeterminacy methods of John Cage, William Burroughs's
cut-ups, Michel Serres's parabolic style, and deconstruction,
among others — offered a glimpse at a possible means of
articulating the above stated desire to make my work of noise
theory noisy. Using cut-ups and indeterminacy, I speculated
that it was possible to bring to noise theory a means of more
strongly representing noise within the text that did not rely on
an ever growing set of negative definitions and displacements.
Instead of following the established path of other noise re-
searchers (Kahn, Kosko, Hegarty, Hainge, Schwartz, along with
Frances Dyson, Benjamin Halligan, Salomé Voegelin, Joanna
Demers, Brandon LaBelle, Jacques Attali, and others), I sought,
in applying indeterminate and cut-up methods, to establish
a novel line of noise research to see what might possibly be
learned from a noisy noise project, from a textual experiment
that went beyond my individual control or intention and thus
beyond what I could potentially conceive about noise without
the assistance of the methods.

To further develop the methodology, I brought
together examples and forerunners in alternative and avant-
garde knowledge production. The indeterminacy and openness to noise of John Cage set the specific program — though I
used an online random number generator rather than dice or
I-Ching tables to generate my indeterminacy. I applied to my
thinking the collage practices of Dada, the merz art of Kurt
Schwitters, and the multimedia cut-ups of William Burroughs

tolerances/affordances that humans seem to have for noise in various
forms. The audio is accessible here: https://deltabrainwavesociety.band-
camp.com/album/bruit-jouissance, and video is accessible here: https://
www.youtube.com/playlist?list=PLS6PKCS99i-8ByNYcu7gqnCSVwb65X-
4Lj.

for their juxtaposition of unrelated fragments into expertly crafted works of multimedia art that brought out of the text voices and thoughts that were not manifest in their original contexts. The automatic writing and the games of the Surrealists and the *détournement* practices of the Situationists further offered models of getting at ideas of noise that were below the surface level of my conscious academic thinking. The research methods and practices of 'pataphysics suggested a means of looking into the particular rather than the general—an arena where everything is marked as distinct and incommensurable by its noise—and the heterology of Georges Bataille was a theoretical precedent for connecting the analysis of heresy, waste, excess, and the excremental—topics that are examples of noise or maintain relations of noise. The ecological thought of Timothy Morton connected both the content of noise to the normative positions on addressing coexistence and being-as-noise, as well as provided a theoretical support for the foreground/background division inherent in noise research. The schizoanalysis developed by Gilles Deleuze and Félix Guattari and the disruptive politics and manifesto writing of groups such as Tiqqun and the Invisible Committee were theoretical models for thinking and exegizing the noise of the collected fragments. For presentation styles, I followed the examples of the quotation methods of Walter Benjamin, especially with *The Arcades Project*, the methods of Roland Barthes' *Roland Barthes*, the methods of Jacques Derrida's *Glas*, the art from cracked media by artists like Christian Marclay and Yasunao Tone, the diverse noise practices of musicians like Throbbing Gristle and Merzbow. And finally, as a means of providing the final warrants for my experimental practices, I adopted and adapted the theory-based textual sampling and remixing of Mark Amerika and the heuretics of Gregory Ulmer. It was not a comprehensive list—practices of alternate forms of research and expression have a long history within the avant-garde movements of multiple art forms—but it was a means of recognizing common elements to the practices. Underlying each of these practices, to greater and lesser degrees, I found lurking the concept of noise. Whether it is the disruptive sonic noise of the music of Merzbow and Throbbing Gristle or the juxtapositional noise of collage, cut-up, and remix, or the noise of the heterogeneous in Bataille, the Surrealists, the Situationists—there is noise underlying the elements that define these movements as progressive, transformative, and avant-garde. These reinforced my desire to move forward with the experimental project.

█████ The combination of the theories and practices of John Cage, Mark Amerika, and Gregory Ulmer provide the clearest justification for the experiment and formed the basis of both my desire to undertake the project and the final form that the project took on. John Cage set the example for textual production based on determinate indeterminacy—that is to say, with regard to this project, a textual production that drew from a specific number of fragments from a specific list of fragments but did so by random and indeterminate means (an online random number generator). The most direct antecedents are the textual components of "Mureau"[41] and "Muoyce"[42] projects, where John Cage collected every reference to music and sound in the writings of Henry David Thoreau and James Joyce, respectively, subjected the order of those fragments to chance, and presented them accordingly. The value for Cage was in the experiment itself and the results were secondary.

█████ Mark Amerika set the model for the next phase of the project. The raw experimental data is interesting and suggestive, but it does not develop arguments or present coherent theses. While I could have justified the experiment as nothing more than an effort to see what might happen *à la* Cage, the text was reworked into a theory remix to develop clear and supported arguments. The textual fragments were not reor-

---

41 John Cage, "Mureau," in *M: Writings '67–'72* (Middletown: Wesleyan University Press, 1973), 35–56.

42 John Cage, "Muoyce (Writing for the Fifth Time Through Finnegan's Wake)," in *X: Writings '79–'82* (Middletown: Wesleyan University Press, 1983), 173–87.

dered or recut, but instead there were significant cuts of the data and additions to the text that used it as the source for a textual remix. This drew heavily from the model that Mark Amerika presented in *remixthebook,* his own textual theory remix project focusing on the value of performing textual theory remix projects.[43]

██████ Gregory Ulmer's theories and methods provide further theoretical support to the warrant of this textual experiment, specifically in the normative positions it claims can result from a reframing of noise. Both Ulmer's associative and conductive heuretics methods and his explanation of what he terms the "CATTt,"[44] the underlying structure of manifestos, were applied. This text is a manifesto for a certain understanding and practice of noise and, following the CATTt, it is in contrast to other forms of noise research, setting itself up as analogous to both the composition practices of noise music and art and a positively envisioned practice of contextomy.[45] It samples, it cuts, it modulates, and it post-processes. The text enacts Michel Serres's theory of the parasite in its reliance on and adaptation, interruption, and disruption of academic noise discourse. It specifically targets politics not in the vein of noise abatement policies but as a method for changing the political status quo, especially with regard to coexistence. The tale is the result of the experiment itself, presented below.

██████ As mentioned above, the tale of this manifesto is self-contradictory. As a manifesto, it declaims with certainty. As a text developed as and then from a Ph.D. dissertation, it

██████

43 Mark Amerika, *remixthebook* (Minneapolis: University of Minnesota Press, 2011).

44 "C = Contrast (opposition, inversion, differentiation); A = Analogy (figuration, displacement); T = Theory (repetition, literalization); T = Target (application, purpose); t = Tale (secondary elaboration, representability)" (Ulmer, *Heuretics,* 8).

45 Contextomy, or quote mining, is a method of quoting out of context that is generally disparaged and considered a logical fallacy. However, for this work contextomy was implemented as a research method for its generative potential, as an enacting of noise.

declaims with the authority of research. And yet, as noise, the work is defined by its uncertainty and indeterminacy. It casts doubt on the very idea of authority, research on the topic of noise, and even the ability to know what noise is in any specific sense. While this contradiction is generally the type that academic work seeks to avoid (when possible), it also forms an essential aspect of our understanding of the relational nature of noise-as-such (so far as we can come to know or articulate the concept of noise-as-such).

█████ In order to generate the text to function as the tale, I developed the methodology of the experiment to combine elements of many of the above methods of alternate grammar and discourse. I sought to remove (with indeterminacy, cut-ups, collage, and merz) the limitations that a more straightforward, academic approach might place upon the textual fragments in an effort to allow for the randomized juxtapositions to provide unexpected insights and understanding. I followed the example of Walter Benjamin[46] in presenting the quotes without quotations or direct attribution in order to remove the impediments to reading that were caused by the constant opening and closing of quotations marks, the excess of ellipses, and the opening and closing of square brackets that marked editorial insertions and changes, as well as to allow my thoughts and the thoughts contextomically mined and repurposed from others to blend and mix in a manner that sought to fully exploit the textual noise. All the texts that I quoted are listed in the List of References section at the close of the text, but not all of the quotations that went into the raw text remain (whether in whole or in part) in the final text. To edit the project, I asserted a level of authorial control, rather than following a programmatic editing process or simply letting the text stand, as John Cage did with "Mureau" and "Muoyce." I read through the text multiple times, highlighting particularly resonant pas-

█████

46 Walter Benjamin, *The Arcades Project,* trans. Howard Eiland and Kevin McLaughlin (Cambridge: Harvard University Press, 2002).

sages and juxtapositions and followed up on and expanded those passages. Then I cut out passages that contradicted or overly distracted from those points. I took the example of the merz project of Kurt Schwitters (and the Merzbow project of Masami Akita—the name is a direct homage) as the justification of my attempts to assemble an incomplete and noisy work of art/theory from decontextualized and often unrelated fragments. Their methods provided guidance in crafting a form of coherence, that is to say, a measure of theoretical consistence and clarity of discourse such that this text is readable as an academic argument and not just a randomized assemblage of quotations. The editing did change the text from being one where meaning could only be extracted in small parts and by chance (again I point to "Mureau" and "Muoyce") to one that has a distinct (if nonstandard) philosophy. But had it remained a project that contained no message save nonmessage, no sense save the articulation of nonsense, no signal save the acknowledgment of its absence, it would likely not have qualified as a dissertation or the present monograph and, as the goal is to further my arguments for noise as a generative method, the work is better served (as will become obvious through reading) by the acknowledgment of the failure of the noise of the text to ever fully be noise-as-such. The Afterword offers further reflection on those choices and a consideration of their efficacy.

Towards Other Worlds Than These   The question that drives this text, that necessitates this textual experimen, is not the (incomplete/unanswerable) "what is noise?" but rather the (normative) "what can noise do? what can we do with our noise?" Specifically, I have directed this project at the political questions of coexistence (with the human and the nonhuman alike) and ecology (primarily drawn from the theories of Timothy Morton and Michel Serres), as these are topics of immediate global importance. The epistemic/ontological question of noise is one that has been pursued by other authors and thinkers (Hainge, Hegarty, Kahn, Voegelin, Dyson, Attali, Serres, Schafer, and others) within noise studies. Their work is what this one is literally built from. But, in building on their epistemic and ontological studies, this work is designed to address the noise of everyday life by interrogating the practical realities of noise politics through noise rather than the impossible project of defining noise without defining it as a noise-for.

█████ It must be stated here that, following any conventional understanding of the concept, this text does not necessarily "make sense." This is a work that was composed through chance methods and interruptive insertions. As such, it challenges sense. This is not to undercut the text but rather to frame it. Sense, in works claiming a singular authorial message, is already a fraught concept that is based on consensus guarantees and paradoxes, the interrelation between language, intent, and context (cf. Nietzsche and Deleuze). Sense is riddled through with nonsense. This text does not deny that it contains its own critique, that it (cf. Derrida), too, will self-deconstruct. Rather, this text sought the contrary to sense. It sought the sense within nonsense, to carve out a signal from the noise. Indeed, given the pattern-making propensity of humans, sense will be made of this text by those who read it. Though the juxtaposition of fragments was random, the connotations and denotations that resulted from those chance encounters—examples of the generative capacity of noise—formed the basis of the text's cyclical arguments. Because of the nature of its construction, this text is set apart by the unexpected and potentially useful insights—notably the rethinking of human ontology within a lens of being-as-noise as a means of reframing the debates around anthropogenic climate change and political equality—that are allowed by the methodology. The author function of this text is undoubtedly schizophrenic, in that it is the product of multiple authors arguing divergent points simultaneously, and the sense drawn from the work is a chimera of the assemblage and the echoes of the primary sources the fragments were carved from. But that does not prevent the text from articulating a distinct and singular position. It acknowledges the fragmentary nature of its (de)construction and the death of its author (function), staging its deconstruction in reverse. While reading habits may lead us to treat the core text as if it had a single author expressing a univocal intention, keeping an eye out for the sutures and seams of the text and allowing certain sections to read as poetry, as existing for the sound and evocative potential of the language, are strategies that I would recommend to supplement traditional academic approaches to the text. These strategies allow for the text to function as the poetic noise experiment that it strives to be, but still offer the potential for deepening one's understanding of noise and its potential uses.

Any errors that remain are mine, whether present in the original samples or in my remixed additions.

Here begins the quoted text.

METHODS I:
DEVELOPING THORYBOLOGY

████ The only threats from noise are oblivion and interruption—one of the fundamental devices of all structuring.[1] The goal of this text is to work towards interruption and away from oblivion, to use noise to interrupt the possibility of domination towards oblivion or erasure (a looming political reality). In that effort, along that path, the text will give rise to several theories and hypotheses. These competing theories will rise to the surface of the text as it meanders in a semi-cyclical and repetitive manner only to once again submerge and then possibly reemerge later on. The experimental nature of this textual production meant never knowing the results in advance.

████ The cracks, edges, fissures, noise, and renegade flows in thought processes, hidden by streamlined or mainstreamed views, methods, and dissemination techniques, are often rendered visible by such experimental actions. It was the goal of this experiment to render visible (or, more appropriately,

████

1 But what *is* interrupting? Is not a vector required before a digression can be recognized? And threats to whom and who is threatening? Are we, as humans, the threat, the threatener, or the threatened? Perhaps a nonuniform admixture.

audible) the cracks and fissures within the concept of noise, a concept defined through its cracks and fissures. The notions pulled from these formations of knowledge are indications and symptoms for a theory (hereafter, thorybology), rather than for a dogmatic or apologetic position of the problem of noise experimentation. This project seeks to use noise against dogma, against the systemization of knowledge. And yet it must not seek to systematize itself, to present its articulation of noise as *the* articulation of noise. This text and the theory it generates (and that generates it) will always remain provisional, indeterminate, incomplete. Rather, this text is guided by the assumption that those that seem diffuse and disparate are linked as elements of a synthesis, but a synthesis that is less concerned with certainty and instead focused on pragmatic results. Without noise, no real creativity. With it, no tight system or consummate human control.[2] Noise, especially in its most effective political articulations, is as a bulwark against the constraints of control (both internal and external) rather than a claim for complete chaos and the breakdown of all systems of meaning and communication. This is a consideration that is often ignored or absent from conventional understandings of noise and its related concepts and will bear repeating.

██████ Noise, as pursued and interrogated by this experimental project, desires to disarticulate, unstitch, or undermine form. That is not to say that this text is without form. As a matter of necessity, it conforms significantly to the rules and guidelines that define an experimental Ph.D. dissertation such that it was able to qualify as one — though modifications have

██

[2] This is, of course, an impossible choice. One cannot choose creativity over control or vice versa. They exist in an uncertain equilibrium. Certain systems offer more control and others more noise and individuals maintain preferences for systems that mark the balance in terms that they find favorable. As should be apparent given the form and content of this text, I prefer a system with emphasis on creativity and noise and a limitation on efforts toward control but, as should also be apparent, I do not favor the complete abandonment of control or structure in the favor of a constant impenetrable noise state.

since been made. However, even in possessing *a* form, it will argue against the necessity of specific forms, of formalism. Noise provides a metaphor for the *as if* of all that is possible yet unthought. Thus noise, as the content of this work of experimentation, also provides the theoretical framework that suggests its anti-formal possibility.

▮▮▮▮▮ Is this question of noise as disarticulation of form a deliberate misreading of a concept colloquially accepted as simply some version of unwanted or unacceptable sound? Perhaps. This text is based on a distinct process of misreading and quoting out of context (a practice also known as contextomy) as well as an expansive multi/interdisciplinary understanding of "noise." Noise, as it is provisionally understood here and following, exposes the nonsense in every articulation of sense, but, more relevant for this text, the sense in every nonsense. Noise may seem free to be anything because it cannot be definitively defined as any single thing—its ontology is particularly fraught—but is this part of the ontology of noise or the limitations placed on the concept by ordinary language? Instead, this text highlights the possibility that noise is able to interrupt seemingly fixed and constrained systems of meaning and knowledge, because it exists outside them as ground and remainder. In this sense, noise must strive, by way of the concept, to transcend its concept, to undermine, to change the focus of a remark, of a performance, of a body, in order to reverse altogether the enjoyment (*jouissance*) we might have taken in it, the meaning we might have given it.

▮▮▮▮▮ Noise indicates the untruth of identity—the fact that the concept does not exhaust the thing conceived. Indeed, noise, as a concept, highlights this breakdown in a manner that is more elusive in other philosophical concepts. It is thus readily discerned that any conception of noise is inherently limited in its descriptive capacity. Noise is always noise, is always disruptive, even in its own definitions and conceptual framework. There are always exceptions, limits, or caveats to any specific definition of noise. Any single or singular definition of noise is exhausted before describing any noise-as-such, but echoes of the definitions remain present, dormant, even as the noise-as-such continues on, indifferent to our attempts to grasp it in thought.

███ The architecture of composition in this text is based in repetition, change, improvisation, nonobjectivity, and contamination. It involved mixing new pages with older writing, cutting up everything to write an as-yet-unimagined future. Perhaps in places, certain fragments seem to follow one another by some affinity— tracing the possibilities of those affinities (as evidenced in the Introduction and Afterword) was a prime motivation for the experiment. But the important thing is that these little networks are not connected, that they not slide into a single enormous network which constructs the structure of the text, its meaning.[3]

███ Beginnings: let us digress for a moment; let us begin with a swerve (*clinamen*). Noise is marked and remarked by digression and this text is no exception. This text is not designed to function as an authoritative articulation of noise, a singular or final definition of an elusive concept. Instead, this text is directed at (current or future) practitioners as a how-to book, helping them to find their bearings once they are bogged down in noise, attempting to find patterns, meaning, and coherence in a world indifferent to human convention. Constructing a discourse in this fragmentary manner presents an intriguing problem: How do you find the words (on noise) that are not there? How do you find a noise that cannot exist because there is no noise-as-such, universally or even provisionally agreed upon? How do you make meaning from the meaningless and, once having done so, how do you justify the foundations of that meaning? The effort to contextualize noise is thoroughly

---

███

3   There is no single univocal position articulated in this wilderness. Nor, obviously, can there be whether such a pattern is apophenically recognized or not. While my editorial additions and subtractions do craft this text towards specific positions on noise, noise politics, noise theory, and being-as-noise, my positions continue to grapple with the quoted fragments and the vectors of thought they retain.

alive and extremely changeable. What escapes theorization on noise (including even this experiment) is the impossibility of fixing, once and for all, noise in theory or practice. Even this text, despite its desire and attempts to leave the question and definition of noise open and in flux, will succumb to its limitations, to its formal constraints, and necessarily put forth a constrained and incomplete noise.

▮▮▮▮ Noise is an anti-teleological project; it can never reach an end, is continually in motion and flux, resisting fixity just as the residues of a dream world. The project is thus to learn to write with patterns that function more like music than like concepts (especially the fragmentary remixed assemblages of noise music). It will present its concepts arranged, like poetry, for their generative possibility rather than attempt to pin them down like a butterfly in a collection. This project may never be understood or approach conventional models of understanding. That is a risk of any project in experimental and avant-garde poetics. But misunderstanding need not be feared. Misunderstanding and misrecognition have the potential to generate unthought and unimagined futures. The noise poetics articulated here reclaim (or seek to) misunderstandings (misrecognitions, misquotes, mistakes) as essential to its generative project.

▮▮▮▮ How valid is this experiment or its possible conclusions? The validity of the conclusions is borne out in the efficacy of the project and its ability to open up new lines of thought and flight. The implications of moving from content orientation to problem orientation are profound. Consider the inversions of conventional philosophy in favor of a discourse as a differential field of issues, gaps, and struggles. If philosophy is to remain true to the law of its own form, as the representation of truth and not as a guide to the acquisition of knowledge, then the exercise (or disarticulation) of this form — rather than its anticipation of knowledge — must be accorded due importance. Thorybology, the study of noise, must be as concerned with the form of its pronouncements as it is with their content. Now that thorybology has been defined, has emerged, it occupies, must continue to occupy, a fecund zone of indiscernibility. Now the truly important thing is to apply thorybological thinking and methods to discover the conditions of life, including those forms and articulations of life that provide the means for coexistence with human and nonhuman others, because we wish to deliver ourselves from the stranglehold of knowledges that root us in the world under fixed authority.

This work, in its effort to be noisy, to incorporate diverse noises on noise, has to develop to the highest degree the art of citing without quotation marks. It knowingly appropriates and mangles the work of others — many, but not all, are works on noise — and presents them (with the assistance of indeterminate processes) as the seeds of thorybology. Its theory is intimately related to that of montage. Noise is not singular but legion. Thorybology is unified but not unitary, because the theory is also intimately occasional; its axioms are semi-stable, but the practice of the theory is utterly dependent on the material available at any given time and revisable upon the availability of new material. Thorybology is a theory for what happens in confusion, when the path forward isn't obvious. The gambit is that if we construct a place for an insight to appear, it will come. The goal: to cultivate fields where, until now, only madness has reigned. Thus the present text is a speculation on the making of a noise into a theory and praxis prototype: thorybology.

How does one who does not know make theory about a concept that cannot be fully or completely known? Carefully. I do not mean to imply that the way forward will be harmonious or easy. How could it be, courting dissonance as it does? The way forward and the theory to map the way are found by playing the game. Without the proven result of a previously made methodology as a foundation, this text must prove the value of its own result. The resulting writing itself is often improvisational, nomadic, and surfing on the elliptical edge of its own possibility. It is no longer a blank slate seeking a pure or purified definition, but an experimental chamber containing yet other chambers, often unusable, and displaying too much tendency toward uncertainty. In its most effective articulations, this text abandons restricted forms of knowledge and knowledge production and replaces them with explorative methods, makes usable lost connections of meaning for the new crossroads of thought. When improvising, form is not important. Flux is. This is an intentional point of the text in this case, an example of its noise and the possibilities therein. It is also, however, proof that one should never trust what writers say about their own writings.

METHODS II:
THINKING THE ANTHROPOCENE[1]

███████ Failure to follow the rules within the aesthetic and academic realms leads to precisely the same result as refusal to adhere to them elsewhere within society. Often: punishment, dismissal, repression. However, the breaking of rules is also necessary for development, for the pursuit of the new. Thus, in certain instances, failure is positive, progressive. Ideas improve. The play of language participates in the improvement. Plagiarism is necessary. Progress implies it. Plagiarism embraces an author's phrase, makes use of his expressions, erases one idea, and replaces it with another idea, with new context, new vectors of thought. This work uses the work of others, randomly

---

1   The Anthropocene—a concept advanced first by Paul Crutzen—is the proposed term for the current geological epoch. As its name suggests, the epoch (climatically, geologically, etc.) is now sufficiently changed by the actions of humanity (by the burning of fossil fuels and the use of nuclear materials, especially) that it is recognizable in the stratigraphic record. The term also applies to thinking broadly about the position and role of humanity in relation to the planet and life on the planet. It is the contention of this text that that relationship is defined by noise and only a more thorough understanding and acceptance of noise will allow for a change in the relationship.

arranged and assembled, as a jumping off point, a means of stimulating new pathways for thought. Perhaps the ordering of this text lacks the full intention of an authorial perspective, but it is, regardless of its aesthetic merits, organized.

██████ This is an account of the effort towards composing a certain kind of text: a thorybological text, a noisy work of noise theory. It is strange, because this is not a work of philosophy as such; it is a work of prolonged heresy against conventional notions of sense, clarity, meaning, a heresy that is continuously heretical, never allowing itself to accept even that heresy is sufficient. This work, in its discontinuity, proceeds by means of two movements: the straight line (advance, increase, insistence of an idea, a position, a preference, an image) and the zigzag (reversal, contradiction, reactive energy, denial, contrariety, the movement of a Z, the letter of deviance: a letter I have been marked by since birth, since the assignation of my patronym [*le nom du père*]). There are gaps, holes, ruptures inherent in this advancing discontinuity. Much of this writing is a struggle to address this lack by inventing a new discourse that allows noise to come into the vicinity of knowledge in a relationship that is neither ignorance nor domination.

██████ The failures of this text are apt to take two distinct but related forms: lack of clarity in message and the limitations of externally imposed form. The lack of clarity is due to the character and applications (in theory and praxis) of noise. It is purposefully indistinct, continually evasive, ever in flux. Thus any work on noise is a process of wrangling its subject/object/ concept into semi-stable formations and articulations such that a thesis might be provisionally expounded. The limitations of the theoretical text (even in its varied experimental formations, such as they are allowed by externally imposed format constraints) also mark a distinct failure. This text will never be noise. It will address noise, pursue noise, and achieve a level of noise higher than average, but it will always be read as signal. Linguistic formulations cannot help but be endowed with meaning, whether intentionally or apophenically. The text is marked by these inevitable failures. It does not deny them or seek to evade them. Rather it uses their tension, traces their edges, their borders, their frontiers. Nothing supports the text except the intensity with which it draws on and pushes against itself.

Even though we are not accustomed to thinking of it in this way, the production of knowledge always puts something at risk. The obvious risks of this text are the above-mentioned failures, but there are others, including the tendency to use noise to repress and oppress, to dominate and drown out dissent. These elements of noise are contrary to those that emphasize the periodic significance of spontaneity, uncertainty, creativity, self-organization, and self-balancing powers in the world even as they often exceed our powers to control them. The latter are the elements of noise that this inquiry seeks to bring to light and advocate for, but they are not the only or even the most common articulations of noise. They are, however, a means of counteracting the exploitative expressions of noise. Negative feedback is countered only by positive feedback and practices of regulation by practices of multiplicity, indeterminacy, and differentiation.

Unlike more conventional philosophical approaches that assimilate only those phenomena that can be rendered commensurable — via abstract conceptualization or categorization — thorybology addresses what remains noisy, heretical, heterogeneous, constitutively inassimilable within general cognitive systems, whether they are advanced philosophical speculations or common sense. Thorybology haunts the margins of philosophy, gnosis, mysticism, science fiction, and even religions. Instead of telling us what its objects of study mean, thorybology show us how we might use them to think. Thorybology seeks a genuinely weird way of thinking, a weirder thought. The interactions of a thorybological inquiry are dynamic and continuous, with feedback and feedforward loops connecting different levels with each other and cross-connecting machine processes with human responses. But far from simply juxtaposing these variables, thorybology multiplies their reciprocal relations through one of them as a factor, and precisely here through noise. The search for order, rigor, and pattern is by no means abandoned. How could it be? Our very nature demands the constant interplay of order and disorder, noise and signal. The questions of thorybology instead concern application: how to turn abstract principles of noise into action, into a progressive politics of interruption.

What is involved is, naturally, something quite complex: it uses the productive relationship between theory and practice, adapting experimental art strategies to the exploration of theoretic questions for formal and physical experimentation. It makes use of the cut-ups, the fold-ins, the collaborations to disrupt conventional expressions of authority and control in order to foster an environment capable of generating novel artistic, theoretical, and sociopolitical formations. Let us follow this trajectory. Everything down to the last detail is shaped accordingly. The question of the subject of knowledge can only be explored meaningfully from an individual position, through the dissolution or dismantling of transcendent structures understood as subversion of power.

This attempt to codify, at least provisionally, thorybology as a field of study revisits the failure of clarity, however. Because of its relational nature with signal and meaning, one cannot know noise while it is noise. To define noise is merely to indicate a possible meaning, which will always be the opposite of another equally possible meaning, which, when diurnally interpolated with the first meaning, will point toward a third meaning which will in turn elude definition because of the fourth element that is missing. Is it possible to maintain a perpetual frontier? Perhaps, perhaps not. But thorybology demands it, benefits from the subtle power of its incoherence. These constraints become advantages, of course, once it is understood that the goal of the experiment is not to communicate, but to provoke understanding by other means.

The point to emphasize here is that the text is an experiment. It is offered not as a proof or assertion of truth but as a trial or test. It plays with an impossible choice, faulty and transgressive, from the dissident minority rather than from authority, from the part rather than the whole, from hetero-doxy rather than from dogma. Thorybology constructs itself, and must continue to construct itself, from the order neither of the sensible nor the intelligible but in the order of making, or generating. Chance produced that rare moment in which the whole symbolic system accumulated and forced thought to yield. Yet this research does not deal with nature or knowledge, with things-in-themselves, but with the way all these things are tied to our collectives and to subjects. It looks to answer, or approach, the following: What is the noise of everyday life? How does this noise, this being-as-noise, think the Anthropocene? How can we more fully understand our being-as-noise? How can our being-as-noise and the thinking of it change how we coexist in the world, in the Anthropocene? In my study, these premises are themselves the object. It is characteristic of philosophical writing that it must continually confront the question of representation. So this text is, ideally, a way forward without knowing where we might end up.

How this work was composed: fragment by fragment, according to chance. Noise is relationally defined as that which ruptures totality, the gaps, holes, and absences in the very possibility of transcendental unity. These fragments and ruptures, however, are configured in thorybological research not so much as an opposition but as a synergistic interaction. The text thus will swerve and digress at times, in the interests of pursuing an interesting idea, rather than delivering a straightforward chronology, in the belief that this will do more to create a sense of the stuff of the theory than a mere recitation of facts could hope to achieve. Following on from there, this text is not only an idea, a theory, but an experience of noise that takes advantage of assembled fragments and the ways they are connected to one another to open up doors to thought that were previously unimagined.

TOWARDS A POSSIBLE NOISE POLITICS

███ Noise is, in many cases, best regarded as a subjective
matter of perception. What is heard as chance, as randomness, as noise, is either part of a larger pattern unrecognized
(perhaps even beyond the machine-aided abilities of human
comprehension) or complicit within that system (the ground
from which a figure might be distinguished). Noise, ontologically, is not just what any one might call noise nor, necessarily,
what is legally termed noise. Not that such an argument would
hold up in court. Legally, noise, like obscenity, is determined
based on the speculation of the potential impact on an idealized "average, reasonable person." To allow noise to be defined
solely through its applications in ordinary language, to allow
it to be articulated only by force of law, is to reduce noise to
merely the articulation of power and domination. The definition of noise would become only what those who could enforce
(with violence[1]) had determined. To avoid that, we must allow

███

1   Violence here should be understood as a broad concept. It certainly in-
    cludes physical violence or the threat of physical violence but it should also
    be read as including repressive and ideological apparatuses that the State
    and the empowered use to control and/or disempower (portions of) the
    populace. Noise (as sound) is certainly capable of causing physical harm
    but a broader understanding of noise (as misinformation, disinformation,

noise to remain, at least in part, indistinct and ill-defined, open and complex, and inassimilable to univocal knowledge claims. With this caveat in mind, proceed, but be wary of even provisional noise definitions like the ones below.

When we ask what noise is, we would do well to remember that no single definition can function timelessly — this is the case with many terms (writing, thought, heresy) — but one of the arguments of this essay is that noise is that which always fails to come into definition. The question of noise, and who has the right to define it, is found at the center of the power struggle between succeeding generations, between hegemony and innovation. Noise is found both in the clamor of the unwashed masses and in the relentless din of "progress" and construction of the new. Noise is found in diversity and confrontation with the unknown, the other, and the strange. Noise is in structures of control and domination as well as in the failure of these systems and their inability to be holistic or totalizing.

Despite these forms of noise, noise is not a consonance of opposites, but rather a troubled unity, a unity that does not synthesize without remainder. A unity that is not without its own noise. This is tied not just to the inability to articulate a timeless definition but also in the limitation on noise being anything, being whatever might be termed noise. The ontology of noise is noisy: fragmented, partial, indeterminate. It is the contention of this text that noise does not have a convenient or consistent place in knowledge-as-such because to articulate noise as a traditional form of knowledge would mean that it was not meaningless or nonsense and thus disqualify it from being noise. Noise is the barrier and boundary, the receding frontier of knowledge as well as the nonknowledge that continually reacts against the codification and stagnation of thought.

---

confusion, etc.) leads to a broader understanding of the violence that a noise politics can be used for or used to resist.

███ The effort to understand noise, to create or analyze that troubled unity, is marked by apophenia—the human tendency to see patterns in random or meaningless data.[2] Humans are pattern-making animals. We demand a certain fixed idea or standard of coherence and consistency in the world in which we live and, failing to find it, we create it for ourselves and wrap it into our narratives. Apophenia is one expression of that pattern making impulse as it is articulated in the face of the meaningless.[3] This text stages itself as an example of the indecision of apophenia—was this signal always there or was it created from a misrecognition of noise? Noise is both the material from which information is constructed as well as the matter which information resists—a further example of the troubling unity of noise. Noise is both background and parasite, both ground and disruption, and undecidable in the difference.

███ This text is explicitly the work of a noisy crowd, a parasitical work, symbiotically growing from and with the texts it cannibalizes for its own purposes. It highlights—because it literally writes with the past, with the already written—the collaborative nature of writing: writing as writing-with. The act of telling is not neutral. What we tell and how we tell it are

███

[2] Apophenia is a recurring motif throughout this text. It may not appear often by name, but the seeking and occasional finding of signals (or what are perceived as signals) in noise is a continual focus of this text and the text itself can be considered a work of apophenia as methodology. Another point that must be stated is that what we do with those patterns that we find is routinely more important than whether or not they are truly "there."

[3] Meaning and meaninglessness should be clarified here—to claim that the universe is meaningless is to adhere to a form of nihilism. It does not declare that the living do not recognize or create meaning for themselves but that that meaning is limited and conditional and the universe as such is indifferent. Naturally, this is a difficult position to articulate in language (a patterned and organized system of human meaning) as it often anthropomorphizes the universe or nature, etc. Indifference is a human trait that the universe remains indifferent to. A further point might be made about who is in a position to decide what is meaningful and what is meaningless. Who decides that an act of pattern finding is one of apophenia? Who retains the authority to determine that something is noise?

political choices. Form is content. In writing of noise, I made a choice. In writing of noise as an explicitly noisy writing-with, I made a further choice. This text exists to articulate its noise, to persuade its readers that noise is not merely nuisance or annoyance but that it retains the potential to be articulated as a political strategy to reimagine our being-in-the-world and an increasingly necessary (in the face of ecological crisis) coexistence with human and nonhuman others. The degree to which it is successful remains indeterminate as to be fully successful the program would need to be taken from theory into practice. We remain at the stage of uncertain hypotheses: **1.** Noise is the inescapable nature of human being-in-the-world. **2.** If our noise is inescapable and a defining characteristic of our humanity, then we must use our noise constructively, creatively. **3.** This text represents an attempt to use noise constructively and creatively, to use noise as interruption and interference against noise as power and domination.

Noise does not, cannot repose on identity; it rides difference, surfs disjunction. It does not respect the artificial division between the three domains of representation: subject, concept, and being. Its nature, rather than being fixable within a specific epistemological framework, gives itself over to conductivity that knows no bounds. Noise is not simply anything that one decides it is, but the conductivity of the idea of noise can be used for anything. This indeterminate position (this nonplace, this *atopos*) is the power and possibility of noise but it is also the danger. Noise does not have a progressive agenda. The arc of noise does not bend toward justice or freedom or equality. Noise, like the universe, is indifferent. Further, noisemakers are not a homogeneous group. This work does not champion noise-as-such (and not merely because of the difficulty/impossibility of defining such a thing). Rather, it champions noise within an ethics of responsibility, tolerance, coexistence, and a process of attunement to life, of improvisational virtuosity, of a liberating intimacy with all things. Noise, due to its indeterminate and undecidable nature, its openness and its oppositional character, forms a necessary, but not sufficient, condition for understanding and coexisting with the other, the unfamiliar, the unknown.

███ As much of this work articulates normative political positions, I now briefly note how noise exists within governance. Noise is legislated, primarily, along lines of power and influence, with an emphasis on convenience on the one hand and health on the other. The multitude of abatement laws that have gone into effect in the past centuries have in some ways mirrored many other social developments—arguments for the safety of workers and limitations on their exploitation going hand in hand with the increasing separation of the wealthy and powerful from the rest of society, physically and sonically. The study of noise legislation is interesting, not only because of the successful accomplishments of it (e.g., OSHA regulations, car mufflers, quiet hours, etc.), but additionally because it provides us with a concrete register of enforceable acoustic phobias and nuisances, as well as who has the power to enforce them.

███ In contrast to the noise abatement, one might ask: What is the political efficacy of noise as strategy? When we introduce noise into situations, we don't know what results it will produce.[4] This uncertainty is good because it's creative, but when we talk about the variety of real struggles in the world,[5]

███

4   This (extra)text is one such example of introducing noise as a creative strategy. The randomization that began the structuring of this text created juxtapositions and patterns of thought that were exceedingly unlikely if not impossible to occur on their own.

5   Vague notions of "noise," "creativity," or "uncertainty" will do little to nothing to solve entrenched problems. These can be either broad concept problems such as equality and universal suffrage or narrowband issues with wide-ranging complications like the current civil war in Syria and its attendant refugee crisis. Perhaps in this, though, it is akin to similar tossed-off notions of networks and social media revolutions. Noise and uncertainty are political tactics; they are not inherently emancipatory or oppressive but can be used effectively in both directions as well as others. Noise and uncertainty are also not end points or goals. Anarchism as a political philosophy and governance policy is not about instability but rather cooperation and mutual aid. However, instability can make for a powerful revolutionary strategy to bring about crises that may lead to emancipa-

what we want is action directed toward a specific aim. In its most convincing formulations, the negativity of the politics of noise is twisted into an engine of construction, and noise becomes a reservoir of rhythmic potential, a parasitic probe beckoning the future.

████ However, just as with any emancipatory potential, we should not get ahead of ourselves. As stated above, noise is neutral and indifferent. It is a tool. Most often, though, noise legislation and noise abatement campaigns are examples of Not In My Back Yard (NIMBY) ordinances that disproportionately affect the disenfranchised, the poor, and minorities by designating where noise (generally measured in decibels) can and cannot happen without addressing root causes of inequality or interrogating the need for loud sounds. Noise as politics, conversely, often ignores the realities of inequality in abatement campaigns and instead focuses on the possibilities of disruption. However, disruption for disruption's sake is not a meaningful or effective strategy. Nor are these policies of disruption the exclusive domain of the progressive. One only has to consider that the term disrupt is used far more often in Silicon Valley to describe new forms of capitalist exploitation than in articulation of anti-capitalism and that gleeful disruption (for the lulz) is the purview of amoral Internet trolls.

████ Reality is holistic — we cannot take a part out and expect things to remain the same. But we cannot expect things to change for the better when only attacked with randomness. Perhaps, instead, noise politics[6] might seek an endless end, a

---

████

tion. However, this is often the mindset of terrorism as well. Noise is a tactic that does not itself have a moral or ethical position. For the purposes of my work and the noise that I advocate, I strive to attach an ethics of responsibility and compassion that would focus disruption on entrenched power structures and not (as is often the case presently) on increasing the precarity of the disenfranchised.

6 Just as one cannot define noise with certainty, noise politics remains forever balanced in a state of undecidability. One must first note that noise is an exercise of power and thus is most often used politically by the empowered — one would cite here the use of noise (as volume or sensory depriva-

lasting apocalypse, an indefinite suspension, an effective post-ponement of the actual collapse, the definitive rupture. Noise is not teleological, there is no noise so noisy as to end all noise, there is no end to noise at all, nor any beginning to noise, or a primary or arche-noise. Thus there cannot be a specific end or consequentialist view applied to noise politics. While this is an obvious limitation, the tactic of noise politics remains a useful tool in a political arsenal.

Difficulties are not, however, mastered by keeping silent about them. They are intrinsic to the enterprise of noise, of thorybology, and of noise politics. Without the questions that I was asked, without the difficulties that arose, without the objections that were made, I may never have gained so clear a view of this enterprise to which I am now inextricably linked. Writing-with noise seemed a simple prospect: perhaps even too simple. Yet the difficulty in creating a text by writing-with noise that establishes and articulates an authoritative position on noise while still refusing to collapse the noisy fragments it is built from into a neat and orderly essay, is not to be dismissed.

While it is risky, we shall advance the above hypotheses even if, for the moment, they must necessarily remain abstract. In writing-with noise, it is what you select, how you transcribe it, express it, present it, and appropriate it that

---

tion) in torture, the LRAD and the use of noise in crowd/protest control, and the in the simple ability of the powerful to make noise without censure and to retreat to the quiet abodes whenever they desire. However, a noise politics can also be described as a politics of disruption—this is not meant to imply disruption in the colloquial sense that it has been given by Silicon Valley and the entrepreneurs that are "disrupting" capitalism with more capitalism—but, as will be indicated elsewhere, a politics of undecidability, power arrayed against the entrenchment of power (the Occupy movement and Anonymous come to mind here). The unfortunate nature of a noise politics is that, given our results-oriented utilitarian political mindset, it is difficult to place a recognizable value on noise politics. If the results cannot be determined in advance (seen as a feature, not a bug), there is no means of offering a clear valuation based on extant frameworks. Clearly this implies the need for supplementary frameworks. This text offers itself as one such, obviously incomplete, framework.

marks a successful experiment. One could object that all of this means nothing, but the hope is that a signal is found (or created) nonetheless. The text does not evolve in a linear fashion, but is caught up in the complexity and circularity of the movements of its fragments. This text does not deny nor occlude that we live in confusion, violence, and injustice. We cannot ignore those unfortunate facts about human society nor reduce them to silence. As the text elaborates below, existence is coexistence — coexistence with the human and nonhuman, the organic and the inorganic, the self and the other alike.

████ There is much more to this noise analysis than a mere shifting of terms, a substitution of noise in the place of established revolutionary politics. Change is nonsense, is noise, is a rupture with and within an existing program or paradigm. In this, change is a deconstruction of a paradigm, an exploitation of its supplements, ruptures, and remainders. But precisely for this reason, noise is the reality of thought itself and the unconscious of pure[7] thought. But that's not the real question. Rather: How do we interpret something we cannot possibly understand? How can we begin to interpret that which we define as meaningless except haltingly, experimentally, apophatically, and apophenically? How we follow a line of thought that is organized by its ruptures and limits and not continuity?

████ Distortion in communication is systemic, but it is not merely a matter of chance or accident whether there is noise, nor is it simply a matter of fate whether one is understood or intercepted. Noise is an intervention at the level of meaning, one that challenges existing meanings and patterns, leading to questioning (and therefore highlighting the attribution of

████

7   Noise precludes purity. All is stained, tainted, corrupted. Every argument contains its contrary, its critique, its *pharmakon*. Ironically, the term "pure" and the concept of purity infect much of the following text despite its position contrary to that of noise. Noise, however, does not exclude its opposites or need to in order to be itself. While the term "pure" (and concept of purity) will resurface in the text, it should always be viewed with suspicion.

meaning) and, eventually, if not always, in the recuperation of noise as new system. Noise questions assumed meanings, assumed structures, normative values and methodologies. This text uses noise to analyze noise, critique noise, and understand noise, knowing full well that such a project is destined for failure (if failure is defined by incompletion). However, the incomplete nature and failure of this project will ideally recuperate as a separate noise system (to then be analyzed and critiqued in turn). We begin with words, phrases and propositions, but we organize them into a limited corpus that varies depending on the problem raised. Here the questions entail: Which sounds do we want to preserve, encourage, multiply? Which noises are expressions of life and which are articulation of domination and exploitation? What is the nature of our being-as-noise and is it possible to articulate a human expression of noise that is creative, interruptive, and emancipatory without being exploitive, disruptive, and dominating? When we know this, ideally, the destructive sounds of power will be conspicuous enough and we will know why we must eliminate them.

████ We write only at the frontiers of our knowledge, at the border that separates our knowledge from our ignorance and transforms the one into the other. Technology extends poetics. Do I contradict myself? Noise is contradictory, even self-contradictory. Contradiction is inevitable in any discourse on noise. These assembled fragments carry traces of their former emplacement, which give them a spin defining the arc of their vector. But noise also contains a difficulty in principle that we must reiterate in order to clarify our own perspective: Noise is neutral. Noise cannot be guaranteed. Noise, as a political strategy, is always precarious. What is therefore necessary is a commentary on noise, an exegesis of noise towards revolutionary goals, according to an ethics based on coexistence and responsibilities over one based on independence and rights. We cannot distinguish if noise politics is strategically paradoxical (purposefully made to appear puzzling, subversive) or merely self-contradictory (a mishap without purpose, an accident). But we need not force the distinction to settle. It is this disequilibrium that makes revolutions possible even as it makes them fragile and difficult to achieve.

████████ Noise cannot be accommodated in any existing category: therefore we must invent and characterize a species for it. We classify information to discover similarities, contrasts, and patterns. Like all techniques of analysis, this can only be justified if it leads to the improvement of perception, judgment, and invention. In short, the sound and the fury never signify nothing or, rather, just nothing. But what the techniques signify and how noise is enacted are indeterminate, the product of particular sites and circumstances, which are difficult to generalize or extend.

HOSPITALITY[1]

And now let us digress in experimentation through a long detour. I draw my argument crookedly, making conceptual detours, drifting in and out of remote subjects, and, occasionally, running into dead-ends. Noise may not be the secret of life, but there may have been no life without it. Noise accepts the risk of being wrongly understood, wrongly interpreted, sanctified, demonized, or else interrupted point-blank, and thus the risk that the discourse can be driven off its course, to inaugurate a dialogue where nothing was planned. I would like to salute the audacity that leads a philosophical utterance to make us desert those dwellings of the mind where reason lives as master, when for an instant astonishment makes reason a guest.

---

1   Hospitality, as it is used within this text, is derived from Jacques Derrida's formulation of the term. It is understood as an openness to and acceptance of the other, of the foreign, of the unknown. An openness without condition to the Other who is received as guest even as the Other arrives without warning. While Derrida did not make the connection to noise fully explicit, Michel Serres's concept of the parasite (which does) draws much of its theory from the same exploitation of the French term *hôte*—meaning both guest and host. The extension here from a concept of hospitality to noise is thus not a jump without precedent.

Noise is immersive because there is nothing outside of it and because it is in everything. Noise is the part of the ontological nature of humanity. We have recognized in ourselves, in humanity, a proclivity for excess, waste, disruption, interruption, and unpredictability throughout our existence as far back as causing the extinction of megafauna through hunting, to the domestication of plants and animals through agriculture, through to the creation of modern technology (especially nuclear), the burning of fossil fuels, and the destruction of a habitable climate.[2] All of these events and more are examples of our being-as-noise. We are not just loud, though we certainly are capable with our technology to be louder than anything else, but inherently disruptive in a manner that few other species are able to address or adapt to. Only recently have these issues been addressed in earnest and then often as unrelated or divergent and competing concerns (thus underpinning the importance of this experiment on noise directly addressing existence and ecology). What this text argues for instead is that we recognize the commonality in these contemporary and historical events and acknowledge the upsetting reality of our human being-as-noise. This recognition of our being-as-noise asks us to go through the experience of the loss of meaning, the loss of control. The recognition forces an existential crisis, but a crisis from which can flow the authenticity of philosophical thinking, a crisis which we can move through and use to reshape our being-in-the-world. It may still be a being-in-the-world-as-noise but not noise as domination, destruction, contamination, and control. Instead, it is an open and hospitable noise of coexistence. A noise that disrupts our own control and

2   The destruction of a habitable climate is part and parcel with anthropogenic climate change and the Sixth Extinction. The Sixth Extinction is the name given to the current spike in the extinction rate in an effort to connect it to the five previous major extinction events in Earth's history. Human disruption of the global climate is directly connected to the destruction of the climate conditions necessary for the survival of many species, of which we may eventually become one.

totalizing desires for control and replaces them instead with hospitality. If I welcome only what I welcome, what I am ready to welcome, and that I recognize in advance, then I refuse to recognize noise, the parasite, the unexpected, and there is no hospitality. Instead, we must attempt to think the thorybological thought, this hospitality towards noise.

No context can entirely enclose a hospitality of noise, as noise represents an impossible excess, an excessive excess. Noise overflows all bounds, crosses all borders and frontiers. No matter what effort is expended, there will always be noise and never any perfect meaning or complete control. The aporia of noise is the condition of this text, but it is also the condition of all thought and communication. The edge-line of the text, the boundaries of what it set out to contain are thus threatened, threatened from its first tracing of thorybological possibility. Thorybology adapts Derrida's account of a hospitality that must await and expect itself to receive the stranger, the stranger as parasite, as noise, as interruption. In being open to noise, to the possibility of interruption, in offering an unaccountable hospitality towards noise, we open ourselves to the possibility of coexistence with the unknown and the other. This is not, as it might at first glance seem, an argument that claims that we cannot protect the barriers and boundaries of our space and our comfort, that we must accept any and all intrusion no matter where it might come from or when it might arrive. It is not argued here that a neighbor's 4:00 am party during the workweek must be accepted with open ears or that the viral or bacteriological guest should be welcomed without medication.

But what does accepting the stranger (as noise) mean? Advocates of noise abatement put forth the idea that noise is localizable, knowable, and tamable. For them, noise is most often just loud sounds, harmful to health and peace of mind, measurable in decibels, and limited by law. This is not noise as the stranger, the *arrivant*. While loud sounds should continue to be regulated and limited, as hearing loss and other health and quality of life issues are worthy political concerns, loud sounds are not examples of the creative efficacy of noise as interruption, as the unexpected and unexpectable arrival of the unknown. This project does not oppose noise abatement-as-such, but rather makes the claim that noise abatement is (almost) always enacted in bad faith — even though there are healthy levels of sound, there is no possible end to noise (even defined reductively as loud sound),[3] and in practice abatement is often the movement (rather than elimination) of noise from locations with power and influence to those populated by the disenfranchised. Instead, this inquiry traces the cyclic restatement of several themes: noise as both creation and destruction irrevocably interlocked, endlessly reenacted; noise as the ontological underpinning of humanity; and noise as a means of understanding and addressing being-as-coexistence. It is the relation of these repetitions of noise and their varying interplay and interaction that provide productive tension in this text and in noise politics.

We now, briefly, turn to the idea of silence. Often presented as the contrary of noise, as well as the ideal of noise abatement (though "quiet" is the more accurate term in that field), silence is a term, like noise, that is difficult to pin down or fully articulate yet maintains through ordinary language a broad range of colloquial uses. This silence, this inaudibility

3   Emergency vehicles will continue to make loud sounds as a necessary part of their functioning. Though studies have begun to show that even warning sirens have become common enough that some people are finding it easier and easier to tune them out. This would seem to necessitate even louder or noisier sounds to continue to stand out or an entirely new protocol for indicating warning and emergency. Vehicles in general will continue to make loud sounds as even electric vehicles are being designed to produce unnecessary sound — that is sound not necessary for the car to work as a car — because cars that are too quiet are both disconcerting to drivers and dangerous to pedestrians (especially the hearing and visually impaired) who cannot hear their approach. Construction will also continue to make loud sounds, as certain practices are often not possible and more often not cost effective to quiet. While there are many areas in which abatement can and should proceed because the project is, by nature, impossible, the gains that are often made are at the expense of other more entrenched forms of social inequality.

that calls itself, that is allowed by, death,[4] is not the contrary of
noise, but rather a companion term. Noise is connected to the
sounds of life: heartbeats, respiration, vocalizations, speech. Silence is connected to thought, to meditation, to contemplation.
And while noise is often understood in a more agonistic way,
both terms are understood as the interruption and disruption
of signals, as marking a void or an absence. Contemplating silence as death, though, thinks beyond the limits of the Anthropocene, allows the possibility of imagining a reality where the
existence of mankind no longer has a stratigraphic impact on
the planet and whether such a being-in-the-world is possible
or whether it implies our extinction. Noise and silence are thus
always linked, always together, always haunted by each other,
by the presence/absence of the other. They always imply supplementary failure, promise risk, emptiness, and annihilation.
██████ Characterized by an intermittent, clanking, juddering,
and halting forward motion, this text is both metaphorically
and literally marked by a constant machinic buzz and whirr,
the sound of the juxtaposition of unrelated fragments striving for continuity (as well as accompanied by a soundtrack of
the same).[5] Its seams and sutures are left partially open and
exposed in an effort to highlight the form of noise interacting
with the content of noise. This is the space and field of thought
that thorybology seeks to open and explore. This experimental
methodology that explicitly denied the historical specificity of

██

4 Silence and death are routinely connected. One might note the straightforward biological implications—a body that does not make sound
   (heartbeat, breath, etc.) is not alive. But one should not forget the political
   ramifications. Notably, the Gay Rights advocates of Act Up used the phrase
   "Silence is Death" as a slogan during the AIDS crisis when being silent
   politically lead not to mere metaphoric "death," as in disenfranchisement,
   but to literal bodily death.
5 See the *bruit jouissance project,* which has been produced concurrently
   with this book under aegis of the Delta Brainwave Society: https://
   deltabrainwavesociety.bandcamp.com/album/bruit-jouissance & https://
   www.youtube.com/playlist?list=PLS6PKCS99i8ByNYcu7gqnCSVwb65X4
   Lj.

its materials and insisted upon their subjugation to the composition produced lines of thought and research that remain
rigorously undecidable. Thorybology suggests infinite paths
to investigate. Its theoretical framework allows the research to
abandon one train of thought to become entranced by an alternate all the while demanding we consider the remainders.

███████ Philosophy has always insisted upon this: thinking its
other. Its other, its noise: that which limits it, and from which it
derives its essence, its definition, its production. In the research
of noise, however, the difference between what is self and what
is other, what is inside and what is outside, becomes increasingly indistinguishable, and any frame becomes a temporary,
easily violated boundary opening into adventure without
reserve. There are many methods that might take advantage
of these violated boundaries. An obvious example is a work
that was made only from references—tangling, intertwining
elements reacting with one another magically and tragically.
The goal in this noise inquiry, in thorybology in general and
in a hospitality of noise, is to see more noise patterns as signals
whether or not we like those signals.

███████ Noise is that which unmoors the world from the il-
lusory fixity to which we tie it down in an attempt to keep it in
place, to separate its elements out from each other and elevate
ourselves above the "natural world," subjecting it to our will
and mastery as though we were somehow separated from nature. By making us aware of our inability to decipher it, noise
alienates us. Noise functions as a powerful enacting of Brecht's
Verfremdungseffekt. It forces an alienation, a separation from
the accepted and established norm, a jarring away from pattern
and habit that can bring about new thinking. We are all no one
in front of noise. We cannot find reaffirmation of our accepted
positions and are offered instead only waste, expenditure, and
sacrifice.[6] It is only after noise breaks down entrenched posi-

███

6   This event of coming to understand human cosmic insignificance
    (relationally to the whole of existence anyway) can be both powerfully
    liberating and damaging. This text follows a certain reading of existential

tions, after we have offered it unconditional hospitality, that it can become generative, creative, fecund. In an attempt to keep pace with the ideas generated, the mind is required to flit nimbly from arousal to contemplation, puzzlement to delight. The results more than reward the mental gymnastics necessary to follow such an evasive prey.

philosophy in this matter and reads noise as enabling radical freedom, and sees the liberating potential in insignificance.

~~NOISE~~

██████ This essay is discontinuous, disjointed, fragmentary, seeming to mark the severing of the relation to the other.[1] It refuses to proceed in a straight line, refuses to follow in the well-marked linear rut. No, it moves in directions that are multiple, multiplied, and stratified. Lines of thought digress only to come back in citation, underlining and inflecting the cresting of new events of language. Words regained, reacting again upon words. Language ebbing and flowing, relaxing into stagnant eddies and contracting again into the wave-crest.[2] But wherever there is editing, cutting, recontextualization,

██

1 While the discontinuous, uncertain, and indeterminate nature of noise might seem to sever relations to the other, to cut and to fragment rather than to connect, it is the contention here that this is the formation of a different form of relation, a relation not based on continuous control but upon heterogeneity that is better served in relating to the other, even the nonhuman other.

2 One might note that the excess of aquatic and nautical metaphors and images are not accidental or random. While the etymology remains contested, it is argued by some (including Michel Serres) that noise has its linguistic roots in *nausea,* specifically as it ties to the sickness brought on by the tossing of a ship by the waves of an uncontrollable sea. Perhaps this imagery is due to Serres's own maritime upbringing, but the metaphor of the sea from its power and scope to its fractal shorelines and its chaotic wave patterns is apt nonetheless.

incomplete citation, there is noise. The whole is also a hole or, following Reza Negarestani, a ( )hole[3]: emptied out by the very thing that completes it. Noise, much as we might try to contain it, reduce it, sublimate it, eradicate it, has the potential to affect us, to pierce us. This reaction to noise could explain why it is that we continually try and continually fail to control it. This noise, this *pharmakon,* this ambivalence. Meaning can only emerge in the gaps and failures of those words that are used to render noise understandable. In light of this, the most effective, accurate, evocative means of addressing noise is by putting the word "noise" under erasure in this text, writing it as ~~noise~~. For the meaning of ~~noise~~ only occurs when the word is understood in opposition to the concept — noise as the absence of meaning — it is meant to describe.

███ How is compositional integration achieved, given the heteronomy of the materials available, given the manifold nature of noise itself? Without my complete authorial control over the text, a pleasure for consistency and continuity is denied or put aside for the reader just as the experiment opens new avenues for thought and discourse. The consequences of this heteronomy are odd, and intrinsically and unignorably relational. Noise emanates, propagates, communicates, vibrates, and agitates. It eludes definition, while having profound effect. Noise is not just volume, but the spread, dissemination and dispersal of its non-message, the poverty and ruination of its materials, the end result of which is uninhibited and no longer distinguishes truth from falsehood, simulacrum from

███

3   One might here take a moment to digress on the topic of whole, holes, and ( )holes. ( )hole is a term that I am adapting here from Reza Negarestani as a typographic neologism that indicates all the inherent holes in every whole. This is similar to my work on noise. Noise exists in every signal, cannot be separated from any signal. Just as there is always noise, there is always a hole in the whole — thus the ( )hole. It is a similar typographic position to that of putting under erasure (i.e., rendering noise as ~~noise~~ to indicate that every articulation of noise in a text always fails to truly be noise).

reality — simultaneously transcendent and utterly confusing because it confounds all previous experiences.

███████ In writing about noise this way, fragments are juxtaposed in novel formations and often will counteract each other, sometimes creating a dense mass, at other times offering more a sense of strata or depths. At every instant, the question of the border comes up. What is a border? And of what use is it if it cannot be maintained? If the fragments cannot be easily distinguished from each other, are they still fragments? In order to identify itself, to be what it is, to delimit itself and recognize itself in its own name, the border must espouse the very outlines of its adversary. To exist, one must delimit. One must distinguish between things, sensations, phenomenal experiences. However, in doing so one creates, by the very nature of division, a marked and an unmarked space, an inside and an outside. This is the origin of noise. To define is to apophatically create noise. Noise is found in the act of marking a division between a marked and unmarked space, the border that is marked, and in the exclusion of the unmarked space, in the rendering of the unmarked space as background from which to analyze and interpret the marked foreground.

███████ In attempting to think noise-as-such, as a readable text, in recognizing it and ascribing to it a signal, thus rendering it as noise, one misses it. The *pharmakon* is that sense of noise which, always springing up from without, acting like the outside itself, will never have any definable virtue of its own. Noise as what always remains irresoluble, impracticable, abnormal, or non-normalizable is what interests and constrains us here. Its divisibility founds this text, its traces, and remains. Noise works to break rules and conventions to free the mind to control what one cannot control, forcing alterations to your patterns of thinking, the content of your dreams and the way in which everyday decisions are made. As a process, noise marks something underway — the not-yet-finished — and this being-undone allows competing terms and relations to be co-present and active in the same dynamic event. It invites one to think. Noise, or ~~noise~~, here works to push beyond meaning and sense, to continue to articulate something even once words have failed or reached the limits of their expressive possibilities. One does not know—not out of ignorance, but because this non-object, this non-present present, this being-there of an absent or departed one no longer belongs to knowledge. I cannot dominate the situation, or translate it, or describe it. I cannot report what is going on in it, or narrate it or depict it, or pronounce it or mimic it, or offer it up to be read or formalized without remainder. I can only approximate noise as ~~noise~~ in an effort to approach the possibilities of thorybology.

▮▮▮ The future of this understanding of noise as ~~noise~~ becomes therefore stranger than the singular imaginings of its past. It grafts. It is a trace, and a trace of the erasure of the trace. The dynamic interaction between noise and ~~noise~~—the very condition that engulfs the text—that enables it, allowing it to be created, provides a conceptual foundation for thorybology. Without edge, without border, thorybology seeks to upset the order of things, breaking down any resistance to thought, offering and requiring no closure but instead an inherent mystery, the structure of chaos unlimited in its capacity to destroy and create.

▮▮▮ Noise compels the violation of its own law, whatever one does, and it violates itself. It can never *just* be noise. In striving to be noise in a place of meaning, it is read as meaning and thus (though an apophenic transformation) becomes meaning, becomes ~~noise~~. In other words, in the face of the recognition that there is no one absolute answer to the question of noise, we must seek constantly, endlessly, for an appropriate answer, for a politically pragmatic answer. Seeking the right answer, or better, the just answer, implies that the experience of undecidability is also supposed to make us live differently. The questions of noise will not be answered, at least not finally in the declarative mode, but it will be used. Noise is a way of being, of living in the world, not a thing to hold, own, control, mitigate, abate, banish, or know in any declarative sense. This could be seen as a limitation of the field, but is, rather, an expression of thorybology's most generative capacity.

What a word such as noise properly means (to say) cannot be known by referring back to some would-be primitivity or authentic primordiality. Noise theory is itself chaotic and filled with contradictions, and as such provides an unclear path. The path, despite lacking a clear destination, remains traversable, redolent with possibility. This chaos of thorybology is an incessant din out of which a philosopher isolates fragments and snatches up odds and ends; no archive will ever preserve the memory of it. Thorybology is not a destination, it has no *telos* or *topos,* but a program for productive wandering. The risk for thorybology is always that its abstraction is too arbitrary, that it lacks the power to properly motivate the amalgamation of found matter within its orbit. Will it be said, then, that what resides in thorybology is the unthought, the suppressed, the repressed of philosophy? Perhaps. In thorybological inquiry, all caution and previous limitations are thrown to the wind. It is in this resistance, this productive tension of the unthought and the repressed, that thorybology excels.

BEING-AS-NOISE

██████ The boundaries are not clear. This is an essential point in the study of noise. For while noise is created, designated, through the creation of boundaries, of lines of demarcation and distinction, those boundaries, those divisions are never pure, are never themselves without noise. The unclear boundaries mark the failure of defining noise, of categorizing noise, of assuring the space of noise actions within a directed political program. Noise is not just noise in relation to something (sound, silence, signal) but the very relation is itself noisy, indistinct, indeterminate in advance.

██████ The Cagean fascination with background noise is key to this exploration of boundaries, frontiers, and everyday noise, given how noise has largely been derived through its ability to communicate while avoiding some contrived message aimed directly at the receiver. Cage's acceptance of and openness to noise, complicated as that acceptance was, marks a significant moment in noise theory. There had been noise advocates before, but, especially with Futurists like Russolo, they focused on destructive, disruptive, and dominating powers of noise — the noises of war, violence, and industrial capitalism — rather than the emancipatory capacities highlighted and suggested by Cage and pursued here. The contradictions are not to be ignored: How can you believe this when you believe that? How can you advocate for noise when you know that it is used to oppress the disenfranchised? How can I not? Noise is complex, multidimensional, contradictory. Noise is not a question of finding out what can be known (it can only be known as noise), but of discovering its emancipatory and interruptive potential, and then enhancing or accelerating what can be done, to react against noise used to dominate and destroy.

This text is composed of assemblages, not individuals, as no single authorial voice speaks uncontested. It is fringed by a determinate indeterminacy, a set of potentials for variation and mutation so that it might continually evade the figure of transcendent, unconditioned, unilateral, and intentional agency—the master-sign of the world, that which creates, animates, and guarantees the stability of creation. That stability is a human construction, a pleasant fable to paper over the flux and chaos of underlying reality. Once the master-sign is exposed as riddled with holes, breakages, noise, we must attempt an understanding. This is being-as-noise and it is the most accurate manifestation of our being-in-the-world in the Anthropocene. It addresses our climate disruption, habitat destruction, and the unsustainable disharmony within which we currently coexist with each other and the nonhuman other. The concept of being-as-noise sets the theorizing mind to theorizing, opening up surprising new possibilities marked by a state of not knowing the answers. This is an uncomfortable state to those unpracticed at dwelling in uncertainty, but it is nonetheless necessary for adapting to a changing climate and understanding our relationship to a planet in crisis. Invention and creativity are not the exclusive domains of the vital or organic—certainly not the exclusive preserve of the human—but are an operation of the world itself. No one has control.

The story of our human being-as-noise is a story of chance encounters, unthought actors, and unconscious creativity as well as a tale of rampant waste, frivolous destruction, and meaningless struggle. Many forces, competitive self-interest and devotion to efficiency among them, have brought mankind and the earth itself to the edge of oblivion. We must change our relationship to our environments, must reimagine how we exist in the world so that we can change our habits and practices. Thorybology, noise politics, and chance operations are not mysterious sources of "the right answers." They are a means of locating one among a multiplicity of answers, and, at the same time, of freeing the ego from its taste and memory, its concern from profit and power, of silencing that ego so that the rest of the world has a chance to enter into the ego's own experience. Noise politics offer a chance to make new connections, and investigate the philosophical conditions that might allow such an extraordinary encounter to occur and echo through time, producing its own fracturing network of mutations and diver- gences. This work forces us (as author and readers) to think, jars us from regularized patterns of response to language, induces a forced, violent movement that reveals glints of future action yet untested, new paths of connections yet unregulated. It traces the separations between restrictions, reproduction, and exclusion, as well as what a noise politics might do to disrupt them. Cage brought this arbitrariness into the open; we aim to keep it there.

The object of noise politics is not to expand the range of entities identified and represented within current states and political regimes, but rather to mutate our understanding and depiction of reality until it cannot be subject to the conform- ing power and the dogmatic image of standardized political thought — for life to become something unrecognized, un- governable, but also something that would unpredictably and productively change from within the constraints of identity and, ultimately, escape from them whether or not we under- stand the next step to be taken. Along this path, we continue to search.

At the cosmic level, there is no causality, no mean- ing, no possible narrative, only undifferentiated being known through the simple fact of noise — the body's continuous hum, which, when potentially audible, guarantees that one is alive, but when impossible to hear, signals the collapse of hear- ing, of the body itself. It is a waste of time to trouble oneself with words, dissonances, and noises if we do not use them to understand and seek to improve our being. With the pursuit of noise, this may seem to advocate for a constant state of change, a change registered in vibrations nested within vibrations, turbulent and self-complicating. This is not the case with my particular research. To attempt to live and thrive in such an environment of constant flux would be troubling, as humans remain creatures of habit. Ordering is the human intervention that creates the meaning and significance of our lives. It is the space where the individual joins with the world and existence through an architecture of silence, poetry, echoes. But the ordering process is a human process, a process that creates noise by designating barriers and boundaries and denigrating anything beyond them to meaninglessness, to disorder. It is this process and the noise it creates that we must seek to understand, not so that we can do away with all order and coherence but so that we can understand the noise and turbulence inherent in every ordering process. This was not conceived by Cage as an embrace of negation, or of irrationality or mystical oneness, or of thought or music with no possible fundamental or resonant frequency. Instead, it is a process of understanding the system as it exists rather than as it purports to be and treating it as it is.

Indeterminacy and improvisation are sources of spontaneity that differ in their respective structurings, as well as in their conceptions of the subject and its relation to the surrounding environment. Both indeterminacy, favored by Cage, and improvisation, as advocated by jazz musicians among others, are activities and actions related to thorybological research and a progressive noise politics. They both form consistencies from their parts but do not unify them in either a closed form or a fixed function. They yoke together potentials in a style of variation. This allows for distinct practices of play and flux with established and recognizable forms. It is noise but it is not a total breakdown of the semantic order.

Thorybology calls for experimentation with both indeterminacy and improvisation as a means of reassessing

how we understand ethics and human responsibilities to the
world and life as well as each other. Cage could not reconcile
the presence of power, domination, and authority with his
experimentation, feeling that they were outside the limits and
crises of his critical focus. However, his model can nevertheless be extended to address the many present inequalities in the
world—the aim of this text. Noise is conceptually neutral but
the noises of everyday life never are. The slate is never blank; it
is always crowded with incipient habits and recognitions that
have to be suspended, stalled, and interrupted. The noise of
everyday life is almost always someone else's noise. This is the
critical flaw in most articulations of noise abatement: noise
is reduced to apply only to things that people with influence
do no want to hear. The world doesn't depend on our categories—our categories are forced and formed by the world's
impinging on us. And our legal categories of noise are certainly
among the things the world does not depend on. Our being-as-
noise, however, is a different matter altogether. Our sonic noise
(from cities and transportation networks and industrial ma-
chinery) certainly impinges on the environments and habitats
that we dwell within (that we are a coexisting element of even
as we designate ourselves in opposition to them) to a degree.
But our noise is also our waste, our excess, our pollution, and
with these taken into account, it is easily seen that our noise is
clearly impinging on the world.

The only way forward is to accept our being-as-noise.
This in no way means to accept all forms of human excess
and waste as natural and inevitable. Quite the opposite. It
asks instead that we accept failure, breakdown, incompletion,
and error as inescapable human traits—in our selves, in our
actions, in our theories, and in our creations—and, with that
acceptance, change the way we act and think about our actions.
We must act in accord with obstacles, using them to find or
define the process. We learn nothing from the things we know.
Knowledge remains unfinished, unexplored, stretching beyond
the horizon of thought. Knowing this, there is a temptation
to do nothing simply because there is so much to do that one

does not know where to begin. Instead, begin anywhere. Begin with noise.

REINHABITING THE EARTH

An indirect approach is necessary for explicating this text, justifying its claims and warrants. This ~~noise~~, this text, beckons us neither forward nor backward, but sideways, into an open field of activity. Into an indirect and undecidable wandering down new paths of thought. Because scholars are expected not just to reproduce knowledge but to produce innovative thought (figured not just as a recombination of good quotations but as opening new arguments and lines of investigation), thorybology is designed, much as other remix theories, to offer a unique means of answering this demand for complicity. It allows a researcher to use recombination as a means of generating new lines of investigations, as a way of interrupting traditional modes of thought to allow for the possibility of opening out into new arguments. This recombination, especially when coupled with indeterminate or improvisational practices, can produce uncertainty, doubt, ambiguity, hesitation, insecurity, anxiety. While not commonly regarded as positive outcomes, these are necessary standpoints for addressing and acting upon the contemporary crises of the world, crises where certainty and fixity have not resolved the problems and, in some cases, have exacerbated them. The process of knowing in thorybology exposes us all to immense discomfort, misinterpretations, imaginary convergences, and forced couplings that, while divergent from many academic norms, elicit lines of investigation and thought that could not otherwise have been conceived. The endless working and re-working which this text underwent, the nagging at a particular notion until it fit in, the progress from an embryo to an often very differently formulated final concept, the amendments and the afterthoughts are the content of thorybology. Thus, to reiterate, I have here chosen to highlight process, to treat form as an element of content.

███████ Misinterpretation is inevitable in all modes of expression. Signals are not pure, but rather rely on noise as both the carrier channel in any transmission as well as the element of *différance* necessary to modulate a signal to produce information. From this point of view, philosophy is in a perpetual state of digression or digressiveness, of interpreting and reinterpreting misinterpretations. This is but one element of ~~noise~~ latent in philosophy. In tracing digressions, paths outside the regular boundaries of control and discipline, thorybology can establish itself within philosophy. It is difficult to know how to directly approach noise. Noise is often marked by warnings and prohibitions: Behold the Outside, you shall not explore it. But to know something means to inhabit its perspective, to incorporate it, to become it, to become one with it, to interpret it. This is not the case for noise. To inhabit, incorporate, become, or interpret noise is to cause noise to become signal, to cease to be or function as noise but instead as ~~noise~~. Of what use is noise, then, if not to introduce some play (some entropy, some information) into our works? In its most creative and favorable articulations, the ideas keep coming, exerting a subterranean influence: fragmentary, primarily in the form of digressions from, or footnotes and appendices to, texts on other subjects. But even in terms of general theory, it is important to recognize that all knowledge is produced by separation, delimitation, restriction; there is no absolute knowledge of a whole. And through every separation, delimitation, and restriction there is the creation of noise, a creation of an outside and background to meaning and knowledge.

██████ Despite an inability to inhabit noise without rendering it noise, the pursuit of knowledge through inhabitation is a component of thorybological inquiry. Thorybology is not simply a field of study devoted to a definitional study of noise-as-such, but rather an (in)discipline devoted to using noise within an ethics of responsibility to reimagine and change how we might coexist in the world. Reinhabiting the earth means, to start with, no longer living in ignorance of the conditions of our existence. This is a primary goal of thorybology and why I insist on connecting my noise research to questions of ethics, politics, and ecology. Thorybology is designed to create concepts for problems that necessarily change, for crises and moments of undecidability. We must question ready-made syntheses, those groupings that we normally accept before any examination, those links whose validity is recognized from the outset. Certain identities, institutions, and power relations are treated as unquestionable reality, even when they are not as they appear. Noise politics would seek to undermine these unquestioned institutions and thought patterns, and scramble their codes as much as possible so as to highlight our being-as-noise, to prompt action in the places of complacent acceptance. This is not a foolproof method, especially if it is not fully articulated. Seen most recently in the policies of many global conservative politicians, the questioning and dismissal of norms carried out without a strict ethics of responsibility can be used to limit freedom and equality rather than enhance them. As stated several times above, noise is neutral, a tool that can be put to use for various purposes. The best way to approach thorybology is to read it as a challenge: to pry open the vacant spaces that would enable you to build your life and those of the people around you into a being-as-noise that challenges repressive norms as it seeks a sustainable ethics of responsibility and coexistence with the other.

██████ With noise is born disorder and its opposite, the world. Noise traces the boundaries of how we have drawn our marked (the world, culture, society) and unmarked spaces (disorder, nature, the void). Thus by listening to noise, we

better understand how we have articulated the divisions and
frontiers of knowledge, where our choices (both ignorant and
informed, magnanimous and self-serving, short-sighted and
prescient) are leading us, and what hopes it is still possible
to have. The future must be cracked open, so that we might
chase our horizons towards the universal possibilities of the
Outside. There is nothing particularly difficult in this ~~noise~~.
The question is not: What is it? or: Is it true? but: Does it work?
What new thoughts does it make possible to think? What new
emotions does it make possible to feel? What new sensations
and perceptions does it open in the body? What new ethics
does it suggest? What new means of coexistence does it allow?
Any new pathways for thought or lines of investigation that are
made possible are a victory for uncertainty, randomness, and
chaos.[1]

████ Writing is organization of data, both selection out of
chaos and, in contrast, turning the object of which one is to
be made aware, to which one's attention is to be drawn, from
something ordinary, familiar, immediately accessible, into
something peculiar, striking, and unexpected. This articulation
of writing is not a way of finding excuses for a lack of original-

████

[1] A brief digression is perhaps in order here. Much of the ethics and
politics of thorybology articulated in this section is based upon a certain
consequentialist ethics that asks, primarily: Does it work, does this act
or thought or practice bring about greater equality, justice, or means of
coexistence? This is a useful but troubling line of inquiry. While the ethics
stated herein are articulated with a specific arc toward greater justice,
equality, and coexistence with the other, it cannot be stated often enough
that these practices and methods do not guarantee such an outcome.
Indeed, one might here note that at present the most common association with the concept "not is it true but does it work?" would be the rise
in so-called "fake news." Whether it is termed fake news, propaganda,
misinformation, advertising, or rhetorical persuasion, a system that allows
for ends to become detached from the means of achieving them must be
closely monitored. Such a system can work well in a society where the public can be relied upon for their discernment but sets a dangerous precedent
in a society where the public can only be relied upon for credulity and
partisanship.

ity, but of affirming that originality and creativity are nothing more than the chance handling of a combination. Thought does not take place without doubts, detours, and repentances. We enter noise discourse, then, by any point whatsoever. None matters more than another, and no entrance is more privileged. Where are you going? Where are you coming from? What are you heading for? While potentially interesting questions, within thorybological research and development, a final and definitive answer cannot be expected for them. Each individual inquiry will offer its own answers, define its own vectors, reach its own conclusions, enact its own practices. So let go of the drive to discover what this text represents, and begin to see what it does in the world. Every concept will branch off toward other concepts striving for answers to problems (climate change, mass extinction, coexistence, political and social equality) that, through ~~noise~~, are connected to each other, and participate in a co-creation of the means and understanding to sustainably reinhabit the earth.

NOISE, ECOLOGY,
AND THE QUESTION OF NATURE

The most powerful forces in nature are loud. At least what we perceive as the most powerful forces in nature are loud. In contrast, life forms exist precisely to the extent that they are fragile. Life is marked by its limitations, its weaknesses, its capacity for failure and breakdown. This is seen in questions of disease, mortality, and extinction, in population dynamics and predator/prey relationships, on to evolution itself and the series of accidents and chance occurrences that led to the possibility of composing the dissertation that this work developed from. While on the one hand we as humans, as prominent noise makers, must make do with this fragility and this contrast, on the other we must acknowledge that the glaring disparity between the human and nonhuman impact on the planet (through noise, waste, excess, pollution, disruption, etc.) requires a reconstruction of the objectives and the methods by which we understand and enact coexistence under the conditions of the Anthropocene. We cannot, in good faith, deny that our being is, especially in relation to nonhuman life, loud and disruptive. There are degrees to which this can be adjusted, but it is not possible for over seven billion humans to be silent. Even quiet and seemingly unobtrusive acts produce, at that scale, a significant impact.

███████ Everything is nature,[1] including the deviations and differences. My aim is not to contest this point; rather, it is to underscore a conceptual distinction and to show its philosophical import. In making the conventional distinctions between nature and culture, between artificial and natural, we set the human as outside of nature or above nature, often in a position of domination towards nature. In breaking down this distinction, in focusing on the noise within the distinction, we can revise our problematic position of domination, as observer of rather than participant in nature. Following this, thought must play a catastrophic role, must be itself an element of catastrophe, of provocation. Thought, especially within thorybology, must force the breakdown of these barriers to action, these preconceived divisions between the human and the other that prevent us from interacting, accepting and offering hospitality,

███

1   While this work will obviously not settle the long-standing debates about nature, culture, humanity, and the environment, it might be valuable here to articulate the position that undergirds the following arguments. Following, among others, Timothy Morton and Bruno Latour, this work uses the argument that there is no nature or environment-as-such. This is not to say that nonhuman entities do not exist or even that there is no way of discerning an external reality beyond sensory perception. Rather, it is an argument that says that there is no passive and stable background that can be called an environment or nature. What is nature? Is it nonhuman life? Which forms? As one gets into specifics, one finds that the environment recedes as the specifics come into focus. As there is no passive background upon which life (especially the often prioritized human life) plays out, there is no nature off in some inarticulable beyond that we can define ourselves over and against. These objects and life forms exist and interact with each other and us but they are not passive and cannot be uniformly rendered as static background scenery. This is the same foreground/background argument that arose earlier in the text. While environments exist at certain scales from certain perspectives, at other scales/perspectives they come into the foreground. The distinction is noisy and in constant flux. An unwillingness to recognize the flux or admit to any perspective/scale other than the human is at the root of many current and historical ecological crises (e.g., climate change, ocean acidification, megafauna extinction, etc.).

and coexisting. The concept of ~~noise~~ that is developed through this work and formulated in thorybology is traced through relation, passage, variation, and invention. Noise is found in the spaces between fixed points and positions, in excess, chaos, possibility, and indifference. It is both inside and outside, flux and play, and the risk of internal catastrophe is constantly present. There is nothing unnatural about this noise (this ~~noise~~), this uncertainty, the lack of control implied by its catastrophe.

█████ Let us not, however, lose sight of the literal catastrophe even as we come to understand noise as a metaphorical catastrophe. To conquer nature is not to change its structure, but its climate. Insofar as climate change threatens us with a danger unprecedented in human history, we need to overcome the catastrophic bias of human exceptionalism that we find in our social and political thought, so as to take into account the manner in which human social assemblages are embedded in a broader ecology. Thus, the point argued here is designed to go against the grain of dominant, normative ideas about nature, but to do so in the name of sentient beings suffering under catastrophic environmental conditions. Consequently, I would like to stay for as long as possible in an open, questioning mode as the compulsion to reduce inconsistency results in yet more inconsistencies.

█████ Thinking (with) noise is not a question of erasing the contours of thought or reality but of folding and thickening them, diffracting and rendering them iridescent. Ecological awareness forces us to think and feel at multiple scales, scales that disorient normative concepts. Thorybology provides a possible framework for understanding and working with that disorientation. Ecological politics is bound up with what to do with pollution, miasma, slime, things that glisten, schlup, and decay. Thus ecological politics is a question of noise (waste, excess, pollution, the unwanted) and noise politics, as argued for here, could be grouped with ecological politics as sharing both content and goals.

█████ The Anthropocene is not characterized by necessity, eternity, and inevitability, but rather by contingency and history. Thus, if we could just get the aesthetic form endemic to the Anthropocene right, we could crack reality, open it up, and change it. It is the contention of this text that noise is the aesthetic form that we must get right in order to crack up and change the contingent and historical realities that have justified the designation of the current epoch as the Anthropocene. Noise is the form of being-in-the-world that most accurately describes the human (in the Anthropocene as well as potentially to our earliest act as a distinct species) and thus the form that must be properly understood and accepted (perhaps even embraced) if we are to escape from the climatic death spiral we have put ourselves on. Since the world is evolving towards a frenzied state of affairs, we have to take a frenzied view of it.

We are surrounded by noise and this noise is (at present, seemingly) inextinguishable. The ecological era we find ourselves in — whether we like it or not and whether we recognize it or not — makes necessary a searching revaluation of philosophy, politics, and art. That revaluation should focus on a reassessment of the value and efficacy of noise as a creative/interruptive process. Thinking interdependence and coexistence involves thinking difference, thinking noise. This means confronting the fact that all beings are related to each other negatively and differentially, in an open system without center or edge. To compose (write, paint, envision, act) ecologically is to build in openness, and therefore vulnerability, to accept interruptions, ruptures, refractions, fragmentations. Nothing is riskier than living in this gap. Thorybology is based on a choice: a choice to distort, to dwell within these gaps, ruptures, and fragmentations. Thus thorybology is taking us into a world steeped in definitive uncertainty.

CONCERNING SILENCE

█████ It is necessary, at this point, to consider silence in greater depth. Silence, as indicated above, is a concept inextricably linked with noise. Rather than opposites or contraries, they are as two sides of a coin. To wit, this text, in calling for a noise politics, is advocating a politics that will, ideally, enable the silence that might allow us to finally hear the cacophony of voices that have been excluded for so long. Just as with noise, silence, as theorized within this text, is better clarified if also put under erasure, rendered as ~~silence~~, to indicate true silence is impossible (at least within the human perceptual realm). Thus, silence should be considered relative and relational within this text, especially as it takes on normative positions. This is a point of contention this text has with noise abatement campaigners, who often advocate for silence when they, in fact, merely desire their particular versions of quiet. Without a focus on the concepts themselves, undecidable and contradictory as they are, a sustainable and equitable noise/silence politics cannot be developed. Indeed, it is this age-old attempt to flee a noise rather than tackle it at its source which keeps coming back to haunt us in this history of sound and that thorybology is being developed to address.

█████ Just as one cannot successfully flee noise, one cannot fully pass over in silence. Passing over in silence would suggest that you knew the shape and boundaries of that which you could not speak, an origin and *telos* to silence. In fact, those who cannot speak cannot pass over in silence, for the poor are poor in silence. Passing over in silence is still addressing an issue, still adopting a position, still demarcating what can be addressed and what cannot. And every demarcation creates its own noise. Noise, when confronted and carefully considered, forces us to ask knotty questions about what we want, what we don't want, and how we negotiate between the two. Noise is the fine print in our contract with the world. It cannot be escaped, eliminated, or silenced. Silence is impossible, no doubt in the same way that the experience of death is impossible (since death takes away the consciousness necessary to experience). By extension, to be silenced is tantamount to losing one's self.

Silencing is rightly defined as a quintessentially anti-democratic process. Who has been silenced? It might be more effective to answer instead, who has not? Silencing, both as a literal process of sonic restriction as well as disenfranchise-ment, have, to widely varying degrees, affected all but the most privileged populations. But just as this text argues for noise as interruption against noise as corruption and for noise as pos-sibility, randomness, and chance opposed to noise as power, domination, and control, this text also argues for silence as contemplation, meditation, and listening against silence as si-lencing. We need this contemplative silence, because without it we cannot hear the voices of others who had been drowned out by our certainty. We must combat the desire to turn our backs on noise, on our fellow human beings, in pursuit of some rare and elusive notion of silence as purity, harmony, or exception.

More and more, it is coming to seem that a life of noise is our destiny, our inevitable, and perhaps necessary, being-in-the-world. We must, however, work to ensure that the expression of noise that expresses this destiny is the ca-cophony of the now audible voices of the previously excluded and exploited rather than a continuation of noise as power and domination. There is a spectrum running from silence to silencing that has to be kept under constant review. The politics of silence and the politics of silencing are not always the same and the latter does not deserve support. Extreme noise making and extreme noise abatement point to the same extreme position: the republic of one. To ethically advocate noise is to continue to ask: Is this noise the rasp of democratic discourse or a repudiation of the discourse itself? and to adjust the discourse and research accordingly. Properly handled, silence has the ability to create disruption and radically alter our conception of the world around us. From this perspective, silence is a refusal to do what is expected, to destabilize established political order. In this, silence functions much like noise, as a complimentary tactic to noise politics. Noise is the sound of revolt, the refusal to be ignored or silenced. It is possible to silence the oppressed but not to oppress them silently. Subjugation must always make a sound. Instead of being against noise and for silence (or quiet), thorybology advocates searching out reasons for noise as well as for silence. In the end, after all the physicists, musicologists, and social theorists have had their say, there are only two kinds of human noise in the world: the noise that says, "The world is mine" and the noise that says, "It's my world too." We need to quiet the first and make more of the second. We need to hear the whole world inside the "too."

Beyond that there is only silence…

REPETITION/
BLURRING BOUNDARIES

For an escape route from the limitations of standard (academic) discourse and common sense, this text enacts a creative repetition, chasing a radical and definite strangeness, dismantling formal constraints, resolving to initiate process but not control the outcome. ~~Noise~~ communicates as information without a purpose—or at cross-purposes to programmatic control and the conventions of form. Thorybology, as a study of and in ~~noise~~, must break forms and encourage ruptures and new sproutings. When a form is broken, thorybology advocates the reconstruction of the content, re-presenting it in such a way so as to make the reader, the spectator, or the listener adopt an attitude of inquiry and criticism.

But let us begin from a different beginning. Any single-theory approach to understanding ~~noise~~ is premature and causes a truncation of our intelligence; it forces us to ignore or belittle parts of the data that might be crucial. Therefore, thorybology is (and needs to continue to be) fragmented, polyvocal, open, and undecidable, not a single or singular theory but a theory of theories. It is not a single approach but an umbrella concept for studying noise, waste, excess, and error. In this work that is achieved through a form of textuality designed not

to represent the world, but to act virally in the world, to circu-
late throughout the world, producing effects by simultaneously
scrambling existing codes, disrupting expectations, and casting
the reader outside the pages of the text to gather even more experiences, thus opening up spaces where new forms of practice
and critique can take flight. This text analyzes noise in a search
for a crack or interruption that can widen onto new vistas and
better mistakes. To compose it, I made use of everything that
came within range, that could be conductively linked. And before I began, I gave myself permission to fail. Failure was, in all
likelihood, inevitable. After all, this text can only ever address
noise in its circling approach towards noise.

█████ As boundaries continue to blur, the question of what
constitutes noise, irrespective of what cultural, aesthetic,
scientific, or legal barometers determine, becomes increasingly
problematic. It is not possible to say what constitutes noise
without demarcating and thus creating an additional remainder of noise. In this text, at least, ~~noise~~ functions within a carefully articulated and programmed set of constraints imposed
in order to generate new forms of art in excess of the fantasy of
singular genius, intentionality, and other metaphysical authori-
ties. Thorybology defines for itself a nonposition from which to
speculate about noise: one speculates only when cast adrift.

█████ The asignifying poetics of noise used in this text,
marked by moments of errant information (but who can
decide which is errant?), simultaneously refuses and exceeds
the imperative to communicate. Despite following programmatic constraints, this text still succeeds in having digressed at
length. But, due to the character of its noise, there is no possible way to distinguish between the digressive and nondigres-
sive, the signal and the ramble, the thesis and the error. The
only criterion of a good tactic is whether it enables significant
success or not. Success here is judged on the ability to write
and think differently about ~~noise~~. Success looks towards the
possibility of acting differently in the world that would result
from this new writing, these new thoughts. The digressions and
repetitious meandering of this text are successful applications

of thorybology and of ~~noise~~ if they go on to produce a new coexistence within our being-as-noise. Nothing is necessarily learned from them, but they allow for the iteration of possible combinations surrounding happy accidents and momentary pulses of novelty. That is potentially enough for notable alterations in the paths and avenues for thought and research that could be used to rethink and reframe our actions in the world. Look again over the edge. The once-overwhelming view of the new frontier posed by noise and thorybology is no longer discouragingly vague or annoyingly complicated.

We are all condemned to silence unless we create our own relation with the world and try to tie other people into the meaning we thus create. This can only work at the threshold of noise, continually working through and against that which seeks to remove noise to establish itself. The overwhelming cacophony means thorybology is significant, whether its potential is for progress or for cataclysm. Thorybology thus comes down, without oversimplifying the point, to a process of selection: filter noise out or amplify it.

NEITHER MEANING NOR FINALITY

█████ Nature is not the primitive or the simple, and certainly not the rustic, the organic, or the innocent. The colloquial human notion of nature, of nature as separate from humanity, from culture, from technology, is not nature. Our noise, our impact, our lives are not above or separate from the rest of existence, from nonhuman life forms, or inanimate objects. In attending to our noise, we might better recognize our connections with the nonhuman, with so-called "nature." One way or another, it is vibration, after all, that connects every separate entity in the cosmos, organic or nonorganic. We must attend to these vibrations, even as they take on an active disorganization of expression and, by reaction, of content itself. That is to say, we must let ourselves be recognized though these vibrations, through these connections, recognized in our being-as-noise, perceived within a relationship of noise, and of aporia, complete with ghost minglings, unprecedented grafts, and insane translations.

█████ This text has cycled through several apparently different topics, but, in fact, they are related to each other, are all facets of noise, of being-as-noise, and of noise. Noise has neither meaning nor finality. When searching for meaning, when striving for teleological purpose, this is endlessly frustrating, and will mark a dead end of thought. This frustration is highlighted by the fact that incurable disgust, pure negativity, and absolute refusal are the only discernible political forces of the moment. These are not, however, the aspects of noise that this work pursues. Instead, this text advocates the abandonment of projects based solely upon a consequentialist projection of their ends and the exploration of interruptive and emancipatory means of breaking open conventional politics and political struggle. This is not to say that the ends and consequences of political actions within a thorybological project would be considered or considered important. Some results are certainly preferable to others; disorder for the sake of disorder is, at best, childish. However, surveying a century in which experience has taught us that man is capable of inventing ever more atrocious forms of violence and horror, it is yet necessary to remark that much of modern thought offers little to soothe, and much to exacerbate our disquiet. What this experiment is asking is: Are their means of exacerbating our disquiet along productive and progressive lines of thought, of flight, of action? Are there means of interrupting the violence and horror to offer a new way of situating the human? As opposed to disruption, which shocks a system and breaks wholes into pieces, interruption suspends continuous processes. It is not smashing, but sitting with. Not blockage, but reflection. Noise can be both interruption and disruption and it is not always possible to distinguish the two in advance. This is, indeed, a threat of actions based on noise politics and reason that noise politics should not be the sole means used to pursue a better world.

███████ Without noise, all we do is repeat. Without noise, there is no information[1] in a signal. Without noise there is no

---

1   Information is used here metaphorically, adapted from the sense employed by Information Theory and articulated by Claude Shannon as a measure of change or entropy in a communication system. More information is categorized as having more change or higher entropy. Without noise, a signal is just repetition and thus has no change and no information. See Claude E. Shannon and Warren Weaver, *The Mathematical Theory of Communication* (Chicago: University of Illinois Press, 1998).

change, no progress, no invention. A progressive noise politics tied to an ethics of coexistence and mutual responsibility, on the other hand, requires a perpetual discordance or interruption, a collaboration between participant and apparatus, in which expression is more important than accuracy. Indeed, the unfettered pursuit of knowledge for its own sake, as if everything worth knowing is equally and supremely valuable, leads inevitably to the realization that knowledge is finally unattainable, the whole riddled with holes, haunted by noise. The drive to knowledge thus undermines itself and its result is a pessimistic resignation from the pointlessness of life. The pursuit of noise, though, does not demand purity, completion, or holism. Thorybology understands that any achieved concept or presentation of noise will be merely noise and it does not run from this realization but embraces it. Thorybology is a theory all the more total for being fragmented. It does not pretend or need to have the final word.

███ There are many pressing concerns in the world today. One of the most significant, as related to thorybology, is the breakdown of the planetary climatic system. The breakdown in climate is directly traceable to the disruption caused by the burning of fossil fuels, deforestation, and industrial agriculture, that is, to the (disruptive, noisy, excessive, wasteful) activities of humankind. To alter this path, to remedy this situation (if such a thing remains a possibility), we must seek an alienation from our established patterns, a reframing of our normal thoughts, a dark, negative, profane reimagining of coexistence on and with this planet. This text seeks to achieve this via an aesthetics and politics of repetition, digression, and interruption, an aesthetics and politics of noise. The text keeps asking that the issue of noise politics be left open (keeps leaving the issue open, cycling back and repeating it), such that any presupposed distinction of noise as valueless is rejected. Noise is not valuable if it cannot be used and it cannot be used unless, as ~~noise~~, it is understood and recontextualized. The weed only exists to fill the waste spaces left by cultivated areas. It grows between and among other things. Thorybology must act as the weed.

Repeating: No longer what does it mean? but: How does it spread? The specter of noise is traced as it spreads, as it infects thought, as it interrupts discourse networks, and networks of power creating little holes, little bits missing, things nibbled away here and there. Yet it is through thought's confrontation with chaos, with absence, with noise, with nonknowledge, that we break the constraints on our imagination and intuition.

To loop and wander is human. To repeat, to repeat as noise, and to repeat with noise and with difference, is the basis of human communication. All knowledge is the process of measuring by a standard. Without a standard (i.e., without any limitation), there is no knowledge. But with only standards, with the exact repetition of standards, there is no knowledge or information either. This noise is not nothing. It is a deconstructive figure hovering between life and death, presence and absence. It rejects the logics of systems that are either theoretically reductive or pragmatically disconnected in regard to their objects. Instead, it asks how one should go about reading such a collection of semi-independent texts, which shift abruptly from one subject to another, try different takes only to abandon them, and do not generally aim to establish a clear conclusion. And answers: We must make connections, establish new lines of thought from previously disparate realms of knowledge. To do otherwise is to remain silent in confrontation with the nature of human knowledge. Remaining silent is grimmer; all truths that are kept silent become toxic.

We are in an ecology of noise, where small effects distort and expand to take form(lessness). Noise is first that which interrupts, inducing a change in relations. Noise is feared, or labeled dangerous and unwanted because it is a transitional and transformative force. ~~Noise~~ is a question of a model that is perpetually in construction or collapsing, and of a process that is perpetually prolonging itself, breaking off and starting up again. Thus, concern with subject and concern with form are complementary.

REPETITION/
ZONES OF INDETERMINACY

████ Frontiers describe what is beyond as well as what is enclosed. Any demarcation of signal is also the demarcation of its noise, of its other, of noise as the perpetually ungrounded, mutable, and self-differing; noise as the outside, the other of meaning, order, and structure. Structure without life is the monotonous repetition of the same. But life without structure is impossible. A continual and constant noise state is not just beyond the realm of human desire but also human capacity. We require patterns, a degree of repetition and routine, to exist, to live as anything that might be recognized as human. Noise politics does not deny that. Noise politics describes a program for interruptive action, even repeated interruptive action against any possible stasis—noise politics is against any "end" to history—but it does not describe an effective program for governance.[1] That is beyond their scope. Governance without any stability and continuity is not worthy of the name gov-

████

[1] Noise is, perhaps, best related to the governance programs of anarchy, though not directly so. The hospitality to noise and the ethics of coexistence advocated above, however, would seem to have a place within a politics of anarchy. This would be governance with noise, governance that

ernance. Instead, thorybology and noise politics seek to blur the distinction between art and life, to unmask the potential for divergence lurking within even the most rigid codes and schemas — a potential that can only ever be dampened but not extinguished by convention — to discover new means leading to unforeseen ends, opening the doors to other worlds than these. This unpredictability requires a subtler and less literal form of noise (i.e., one that takes the form of ~~noise~~) where the interplay of noise and signal persist alike. Aspects of political unpredictability for noise include: announcing the void, voicing insufficiency, refusing recuperation — the important thing in thorybology is to not stop questioning; curiosity has its own reason for existing.

████ To go forward with ~~noise~~, what we require is ~~silence~~ and a deep understanding of the environment. Thorybology maintains a research position that is always experimental (unknown in advance) so that it might subvert tactics based in human-centeredness. No doubt there is a threshold in all matters that must be kept in mind. Thorybology proposes a style of consciousness marked by an emphasis on din and by a re-entry into the rich fringes of sensation. What is vital to our consciousness is that we connect to noises and how we make those connections. Cage suggests a lucid scheme: if we try to disregard noises, they agitate us; but if we listen to them and recognize them, they may permit us to inhabit the world. Noise here crosses into sense — the signal, or at least the strategy of it as it relates to ~~noise~~, retains a capacity for noise — jumps, cuts, gaps, alterations all allow this, hence the continued vibrancy of those strategies.

████ Turning a deaf ear to the violence of the world will not silence it. The only way to address violence is by facing it, acknowledging it. States and societies (as they are currently constructed) are marred by violence at the most basic and

████

was open to change and adaptation, not governance in a constant state of change and disruption — an important caveat.

foundational of levels. In order to acknowledge the violence of the world, one must seek to radically restructure society, states, and our coexistence with/on the planet. Where there is a history of organization, introduce disorder. Where there is a history of disorganization, introduce order. Every encounter is a gamble. If the situation is hopeless, we have nothing to worry about. We had to conceive of silence in order to open our ears. We need to conceive of anarchy to be able wholeheartedly to do whatever another tells us to. To bring the play of intelligent anarchy into a world environment, we must encourage chance and indeterminacy, with a view toward liberating life from fixed structures of control. Thus, we are called not to imitate Cage's actions, but to extend this process into new complex situations, to force connections between the process diagrammed in this text and new contexts.

███████ The world is a moving target to be tracked experimentally in practice, not pinned beneath knowledge in thought. At the crossroads of both the politics of noise and silence, where the outcomes are unforeseen, there is a chance that they could feed forward into something greater — and a chance they might not. Without experimentation, without the production of zones of indeterminacy, however, you are only likely to end up with more of the same. The event exceeds intention, it gathers together the potentials inherent in a specific material situation, implicates and complicates them in another, and individuates subjects and objects through its unfolding. In other words, the cacophony is not silent and must not be silenced.

██████████

THE WANDERING PATH

In the beginning was the noise. In the end there will be noise. Noise is the ground against which all signals must define themselves, the medium by which signals travel. Thus, noise stems from the roots of knowledge, makes knowledge possible, even as it articulates the limits of knowledge. Our unfortunate times (and the limits the times impose on our knowledge) thus compel me to write in a new way, to think in a new way, to write and think ~~noise~~. Because we cannot properly acknowledge our noise or the global impact of our noise, our waste, our excess, our filth, our disruption, and our destruction, I must write in a manner that draws attention to that noise, to noise as the other of knowledge. Such a practice is necessarily incomplete, even as it tries to be comprehensive. But its incompletion does not prevent it from acting, from demanding change in the world, and in the ways we think about the world.

How much noise must be made to silence noise?[1] How often must I interrupt, digress, and deviate through (and with) my discourse in order to force the change that would reshape

---

[1] This metaphor draws directly from the process of active noise cancellation (such as used in noise-cancelling headphones) that generates noise (or rather a construction of expected noise) to cancel out external noise by

the human relationship with the nonhuman? How can I make my noise challenge the increasing volume of waste, excess, domination, power, destruction, and desecration? It might have been better for us if the Earth had screamed, as it did for Professor Challenger.[2] If it had done so, it might have been easier for us to recognize our error. Instead, the world has gone eerily silent. Thinking the ecological thought, and consequently, the thorybological thought, is difficult: it involves becoming open, radically open—open forever, without the possibility of closing again. Knowing is no longer enough, we must also act. We must use our noise to reimagine our collective being-as-noise, to redirect its flow.

The primary source of noise is within the body, whose subliminal murmur our proprioceptive ear sometimes strains to hear: billions of cells dedicated to biochemical reactions, the likes of which should have us all fainting from the pressure of their collective hum. The second source of noise is spread over the world: thunder, wind, surf, birds, avalanches, the terrifying rumbling that precedes earthquakes, cosmic events. These forms of noise are the sounds of life, demonstrating the inevitability of being-as-noise. But they are increasingly too quiet for us to recognize. Humans have replaced those sounds of the body and the world with louder and louder forms of everyday life, of progress, of development, of technology—transportation, construction, war.

We have enormous difficulty in accepting our limitedness, our finitude, and this failure is a cause of much tragedy (for both the human and especially the nonhuman). Central to this is a failure to understand failure, to understand the reality

being out of phase with it. Despite there being more noise, we hear less of it.

2   In Sir Arthur Conan Doyle's "When the World Screamed," an early articulation of what would now be considered the Gaia Hypothesis, Professor Challenger drills into the core of the earth until he pierces its brain, causing it to unleash a horrifying and piercing scream. He does this, in a disgusting articulation of privilege, simply because he can, to demonstrate that he exists and to make the world literally notice him.

of being-as-noise. Philosophy begins in disappointment, in failure. The hope and aim of this text and thorybology as a whole is to open what philosophers most often seek to close, to seek out an unfinished knowledge, to dwell in failure and undecidability. The ecological thought is a virus that infects all other areas of thinking and thorybology, now infected, seeks to do the same. Together they describe a method for finding and making use of anomalies, paradoxes, and conundrums in an otherwise smooth-looking stream of ideas. Meaning arises from the meaningless. Background and foreground rely on distinguishing between here and there, this and that. Thorybology interrupts those distinctions, breaks them down, blurs their boundaries. After all, noise has no contradictory equivalent. The contradiction of a noise is a noise.

█████ This text traces the journey of the thinker who does not have to be contented with canonical knowledge or with the correct proof, but who must throw himself also into myths, stories, and literatures. Who must seek, through these diverse sources, a new clinamen, a disturbing imbalance and fragility that haunts this play in order for it to be play, the irruption of radical uncertainty into all fields and the end of the comforting universe of determinacy. Wandering includes the risk of error and distraction but it is philosophy by contact. This text is situated on a wavering margin between words and music, and between music and sheer sound, and ultimately between sound (foreground) and noise (background).

█████ In the use of a distinction, the distinction itself becomes invisible insofar as one passes "through" the distinction to make indications. The result is thus that we end up surreptitiously unifying the world under a particular set of distinctions, failing to recognize that very different sorts of indications are possible. Only by recognizing the distinctions that we have made and the frontiers and divisions that those distinctions have made, the noise they have produced and were produced by, can we understand other possible outcomes, other paths for thought and action. We are in the noises of the world, we cannot close our door to their reception, and we evolve, rolling in their incalculable swell. Noise is a turbulence, it is order and disorder at the same time, order revolving on itself through repetition and redundancy, disorder through chance occurrences, through the drawing of lots at the crossroads, and through global meandering, unpredictable and crazy. The politics of this turbulence is an anarchism of infinite responsibility rather than unlimited freedom, even though the goal of responsible action might be the cultivation of the other's freedom. Humans are embarked on an irreversible economic, scientific, and technological adventure. One can regret the fact, and even do so with skill and profundity, but that is how it is, and it depends less on us than on what we have inherited from history. There is no exit from this situation, but that does not mean there is no hope or possibility for change.

IN THE FACE OF HORROR

Disaster overtakes disaster; the whole land is laid waste, to misery, to despair, to the pursuit of inconsistent shadows that provide nothing but vertigo or rage. This is life in the Anthropocene. The world is increasingly unthinkable—a world of planetary disasters, emerging pandemics, tectonic shifts, strange weather, oil-drenched seascapes, and the furtive, always-looming threat of extinction. We are beginning to hear it as the sound of our oblivion, life opening out into a void. This need not be the case. Thorybology offers another means of understanding our present crisis. Noise as a truth is negative and we will not establish it absolutely. But through the apophatic truth of noise, we might come to understand other ways of living and of coexisting.

I have not meant to express my thought exclusively but also to help you clarify what you yourself think. As it is normally constructed, especially within the sciences, the intellectual process automatically limits itself by producing only positively defined forms of knowledge. Thorybology, by contrast, is built negatively, assembled from its own waste products as well as the waste and excess of others, thus liberating itself, albeit in a disordered way, to be other than conventional science, to follow the models of 'pataphysics, discordianism, and negative theology.

Let one consider the abyss that is open before humanity: we are currently faced with, separate from but not unconnected to social, economic, and political inequalities and instabilities, an ecological crises of staggering magnitude. Human reflection cannot be casually separated from an object that concerns it in the highest degree; we need a thinking that does not fall apart in the face of horror, a self-consciousness that does not steal away when it is time to explore possibility to its limit. Yet, increasingly, established methods and models for thinking and reflecting are incapable of facing this abyss, of offering a means of plunging into the unknown such that we might emerge from the other side. Thorybology constructs itself as a philosophy that demands a clear recognition of these conditions, which is opposed to any homogenous representation of the world, in other words, to any standard philosophical system. It is only by these means that the present crises are properly understood and addressed.

Unfortunately, this clarity has its drawbacks. In this position of object as catastrophe, thought lives the annihilation that constitutes it as a vertiginous and infinite fall, and thus has not only catastrophe as its object; its very structure is catastrophe—thorybology is itself absorption in the nothingness that supports it and at the same time slips away. It is not really a question of knowing first of all what must be done, but what result must be envisioned. In aiming for an envisioned future, one can articulate an interruptive plan of action. While that future may not come to pass, interruption for the sake of interruption is far more reminiscent of the politics of domination than emancipatory noise politics.

If there is a conclusion, it is zero. Thorybology is not a philosophy of solutions or ends. While it has goals of a sustainable future marked by coexistence and an ethics based on responsibilities rather than rights, on obligation over entitlement, thorybology does not and cannot articulate a direct path to that future. Perhaps such a thought is incomprehensible within the bounds of thorybology. What thorybology can offer, however, is a philosophy of interruption, of digression, of noise, a philosophy that is a call to action, that cries out: Hear, a noise! Listen, it is coming—the abyss created by human misrecognition, misunderstanding, and willful ignorance of its being-as-noise is coming. The cry is both a call to action and the echo of its lack. It is the origin of the forgotten, of silence, of the unknowable. It is complicit with the catastrophe, with the hidden and occulted. It assumes, as inevitable, error, nausea, and the incessant agitation of the possible and of the impossible. Thorybology confronts this horror directly even as it strives to be unbound, arcing towards the paradoxical thought of the unthinkable. Thorybology marks a gulf, a discontinuity from the conventional belief in a world full of meaning to the final dislocation of meanings, of all meaning, which soon proves to be unavoidable. And I say at once that it does not lead to a harbor but to a place of bewilderment, of nonsense.

████ Given the depressing lack of success that other philosophies and political strategies have demonstrated, is it not time that bewilderment gets a chance to prove to be a more effective strategy? Humanity does not recognize its collective being-as-noise. Instead we listen obliquely, as if we were deaf to the sounds of this world, as if we had refused to listen to the cacophonous din of our own organism. We have become skilled in selectively ignoring the world, even when it shows itself to be blatantly counterintuitive or indifferently nonhuman. Thorybology is a philosophy and a politics designed to address that indifference, to re-channel our cacophonous din, to use our noise against itself.

████

——

INTERPRETING ~~NOISE~~

How to interpret noise? Or even ~~noise~~? The interpretive strategies that enable the strange and unique property of a discourse that organizes the economy of its representation such that it is always ~~noise~~, that it remains ~~noise~~, remains in motion, fleeing the rigorous application of meaning to its meaninglessness, yet avoids being or being labeled mere pointless nonsense, are not trivial. The rare force of this text is that you cannot limit it to saying this is that, this is the subject, this is not the subject, this is the same, this is the other, this is noise, this is ~~noise~~, this is silence, this is ~~silence~~. Remain undaunted; these words are citations. They are fragments gathered up because of a certain relationship to ~~noise~~, a certain turn of phrase or poetic language that explicated the concept, abductively linked, conductively associated. But as fragments pulled from previous context, previous clarity, they already resist interpretation, resist transplanted clarity. Only a certain practice of theoretical fiction or experimental theory can work against the frame, make it play against itself, derange all the archival and indexing spaces and condense this undecidable writing into a fixed and semi-permanent form.

However preliminary, a deciphering or interpretation of noise cannot be neutral, neuter, or passive. Even as noise-in-itself is neutral, any interpretation of it will not be. Interpreting noise demands the full acknowledgement of noise, of noise-as-~~noise~~, and thus the inevitable failure of any interpretive project. This is the failure that noise abatement has yet to acknowledge and thus why it tends to campaign in bad faith. The question astir here, precisely, is that of presentation. This text induces by agglutinating rather than demonstrating, by coupling and decoupling, gluing and ungluing, rather than by exhibiting the continuous, analogical, instructive, suffocating necessity of discursive rhetoric. In this way, this text is able to articulate an interpretative process that does not hide from its inevitable failure, that accepts noise as ungraspable, neither grasped nor retained but continually bringing the unknown back to the known, breaking up its mystery to shed light on it. The result of the interpretation is never an ontology of noise-as-such but rather of ~~noise~~. This ~~noise~~ recognizes the fragmentary nature of its interpretation as well as the fragmentary nature of its construction and does not hold these fragments as marginal. Only in the fragments, the citations, the ( )holes, the gaps, the aporias, the ruptures can ~~noise~~ be interpreted, only there, because noise is negatively defined (i.e., by what it is not— not acceptable sound, not music, not valid, not a message or a meaning) and because it is also a negativity, can noise be provisionally grasped as ~~noise~~ and articulated into thought, into philosophy, into action.

███████ Noise goes on. It advocates the possibility of autonomy and self-knowledge through the creative process of reorganizing the ordinary to understand its extraordinary quality and to impress upon readers and listeners how incomplete the world is and how to coexist within it. That coexistence requires a case of reinventing how we understand the role of the human and our being-as-noise. It supports, through thorybology, following the detours of thought to the point of annihilating or rendering indeterminate all the distinctive signs of a prior identity, beginning with the very border between sense and nonsense. The motif of the limit, of the frontier, of the parting line has furrowed the whole text. Noises are not only interference but they tend to interfere at random. They work to transform the limit, obliquely, by surprise, always filled with chaos and chance, filled with every possibility, and as a consequence it is impossible to divide and predict. Noise is the nomadic producer of differences.

█████ Each fragment of this text, each fragment that went into the construction of this text, has its own network with its own intentions, times spaces, and histories. Divergences or conflicts necessarily appeared and new things were made from the conjunction and juxtaposition of these conflicting and divergent fragments. The presence of noise forces us to give up knowing with certainty. Interpretative strategies proceed, then, by seeking out the edges, the inner walls, the passages, the fragments, the margins, the divergences, the transformation to come, and the unpredictability of new knowledge, new techniques, and new political givens, all the better to spark change and create relationships, preferably between all things in the world.

CLARITY

All research into sound must conclude with silence. The future of philosophy depends on its capacity for progressive adaptation to the changing of its conditions. The recognition of the Anthropocene is among the most necessary recognitions of these changed conditions. The Anthropocene is defined not only by the expansive extent of humanity and our (geologic/strateographic) influence, but also by the opposing limits of our understanding, an understanding defined by its limitations, gaps, noises, and holes. These holes, a confusion of solid and void, are inconsistencies, anomalies that act at cross-purposes to a system of order, permit every sort of shifting and jamming. These holes and gaps and anomalies of thought require a philosophy designed for these conditions. They require thorybology. Thorybology acknowledges the looming potential for pathological disaster, but an acceptance of error remains the future. Change, risk, conflict, strife, and death are the very processes of life, and we cannot avoid them. Accepting that inevitability is precisely what clarity is. It brings to light the distinctions that appear in what used to seem full, the holes in what used to be compact. And conversely, where just before we saw end points of clear-cut segments, now there are indistinct fringes, encroachments, overlappings. This is the clarity of thorybology, a clarity that does not deny the conflicts and risks inherent in life, in being-as-noise, but rather embraces them and thrives on them.

Climate is at once an enclosing notion, imagined as the bounded milieu that is unavoidably ours, and a disturbing figure, for it is with the recognition that there is climate that the human species is now recognizable as a being that for all its seeming diversity is nevertheless bound into a unity of destructive power. Alternative ways of speaking about, and responding to, the calamitous impacts of climate change are therefore urgently required, both as a spur to mitigation and in the interests of what is optimistically termed "adaptation." Thorybology is a philosophy of calamity and catastrophe and thus is well positioned to address them in climate as well as elsewhere in society. We live in a world where there is more and more information, and less and less meaning, a world of noise and instability. Enlightenment is not about realizing a fixed and unchanging essence within; it refers to being harmonious with change and flux. There is no longer anything but movements, vibrations, thresholds. Thorybological thinking amounts to a process of interpreting according to a scheme that we know to be insufficient but that we cannot get rid of, that is to say, a scheme that cannot fully account for noise, vibrations, frontiers, and thresholds. But perhaps it is this awareness of limitation that is the most powerful weapon against our contemporary unconstrained being-as-noise and its disastrous impacts to life, the universe, and everything. To once again reiterate, it is always more useful to ask what something can do, its potential, rather than what it is, its essence. What can a thorybology based on limits and insufficiencies do?

The rhythms of the universe are infinitely various. Some are of such magnitude as to be incomprehensible. Thorybology does not denounce any possible confusion, but rather, through its dwelling with noise, becomes capable of inhabiting and digesting more esoteric perspectives. The problem is not that of being free but of finding a way out, or even a way in, another side, a hallway, an adjacency, as escape from what we have accepted as the norm but, if maintained, will doom humanity and life as we currently recognize it.

Thorybology is an offer of hope as clarity endlessly plunges into obscurity.

INDETERMINATE CONCLUSIONS

The very possibility of the emergence of control, or a reduction of potential outcomes, is predicated on an originary chaos or disorder. Cage insists control is "a function of uncertainty." This uncertainty is, both within this text and without, a function of fragmentation. In this text, as elsewhere, we find that society needs to be changed in order to recognize its uncertainty, the path both to enlightenment and political liberation. This is the project of thorybology: to seek that uncertainty, to allow for the (partial/temporary) separation of knowledge from the bounds of already-shaped human thought, and to let that thought be interruptive, not representative or meaningful, but reality-producing, creative in its production of actual variable stances toward perception and action. And unpredictably so, so that it might court each event in its singular unfolding, embracing the fringe or indeterminacy that founds decisions and sensing the contours of the swarm. When questioned, thorybology expects something strange to happen. It expects the unexpected, it welcomes the stranger, it greets noise with hospitality. It is work. It is stitched together from fragments manipulated to such degrees as to leave them abstracted and stripped of many of their original markings but able, nonetheless, to articulate in this text a philosophy and politics of noise and positive change.

Human thought, despite claims and hopes to the contrary, does little to reduce the chaos of the world to orderly laws. In fact, a desire for order in one realm will often produce disorder in others; a concept suggested by entropy and negative entropy in Information Theory and other sciences. Rather than insisting on order or a clear system of meaning, thorybology instead rides the chaos — extremely interesting, always unpredictable. Thorybology advocates a thought that becomes the motor of creation as it deforms the systems of thought and meaning it is used to address, as well as the transmission of noise that stimulates a new system to develop.

Noise is unconcerned with determining how we should act or to what models we should conform. Instead, this (non)politics calls for experimental practices geared toward determining how it might be possible to live, what ways of inhabiting the world might be made possible by and through active experimentation with the real. It is necessarily a creative and productive politics, and it is inherently risky. There is no guarantee that a given experiment leads to liberation or that a novel approach does not fold back onto the grid of existing identities and representation. Instead, it highlights the importance of being perplexed, the value inherent in unpredictability used to interrupt entrenched structures of power and domination. Thus thorybology expands on the indeterminate nature of noise politics to add in a necessary ethics of responsibility and coexistence so that noise, as a process, cannot be exclusively exploited to further disadvantage the weak and disenfranchised.

Without noise, without change and randomness, the world around becomes indistinguishable, the ability to make and recognize distinctions is lost in an endless repetition of the same. Change begins with noise and belongs to the noises of the environment and takes them into consideration. There is no such thing as an empty space or an empty time. There is always something to see, something to hear. In fact, try as we might to make a silence, we cannot. My intention here has been to say what I had to say in a way that would exemplify it, that would, conceivably, permit the reader and listener to experience what I had to say rather than just hear about it, to articulate noise and noise politics and noise theory in a manner that, while coherent, remained noisy, did not lose touch with its animating force. Even the most stable of structures can be made to submit to the interruption of noise so that we might continually develop new capacities for selection, new ways of surprising ourselves and generating new affects, and new ways of engaging with the world.

█████ Thorybology is designed to spark curiosity and awareness, to seek thought and music that celebrate and proliferate the singular rather than the general, that displace comfortable categories and moral questions, and that seek the emergence of the unpredictable, the alien, the disruptive. This is the great lesson of this text in particular and thorybology in general: every situation is tinged with noise recognized as ~~noise~~, as remainder, as something more, something not yet accounted for. This remainder of every situation is the noise that forms the basis of thorybology, the animating content of its research and development. Thorybology does not offer a specific program that is guaranteed to meet specific goals, but what one loses in assuredness of outcome, one gains in the capacity to generate a change far greater and wide reaching than one could anticipate. To follow a plan of actions that does not guarantee specific outcomes, one must accept the consequences, devastating as they, at times, are in order to explore the degree of play within boundaries that exist because the boundaries, as such, are already inescapable.

█████ Here ends the quoted text.

AFTERWORD:
A REASSESSMENT

██████ The first and most necessary question to ask about this project is: did the experiment succeed? Well, yes and no.

██████ The project is noisy and it is about noise (or, rather, ~~noise~~). It is repetitive and disjunctive, it is digressive and meandering, it is at times vague and at others pointed. And by that measure, it is a success. It meets the criteria that I set out: to create a work of noise theory that is itself noisy, that performs in the milieu it analyzes. It qualified (in an earlier form) as a valid Ph.D. dissertation and is here published as an academic monograph; again, success. Gonzo noise research.

██████ But how noisy is it? For that, I must acknowledge that I am not in the best position to tell. Dwelling within this noise, this indeterminate text for so long, I found it difficult to recognize on my own what made conventional sense and what did not, what new lines of inquiry I was drawing from the project and which might have been accessible through more traditional means. I consistently found patterns and possibilities in associated disjunctive fragments, in associative leaps of logic that those who had not drowned in noise and noise research did not see.

██████ The end project is certainly not as noisy as the raw text data, but is that a sufficient criterion? And even that randomly conjoined text is still shaped by the selection criteria I used to build my library of noise fragments. It is not simply an assemblage of possible words, phrases, syllables, or phonemes. In order to be noise, does it have to be as noisy as random text, chase some ideal of "pure" noise? Is that not just creating an arbitrary demarcation between the sufficiently and insufficiently noisy? And, as demonstrated above, demarcation creates its own noise, its own barriers, boundaries, and frontiers. In the end, then, I will contend that it is noisy and that it performs noise in a manner not present in other works of noise research, though the model might be difficult to repeat. Like a hunter tracking elusive and intelligent prey, this model will likely exhibit diminishing returns and new models will need to be continually invented and attempted.

██████ The text, as it was initially compiled from the full 1,700 disparate quotations, did not, and, reasonably, could not articulate specific positions on any topic, even one as multifaceted and contradictory as noise. Drawing, as it did from both pro-noise and anti-noise camps, there were times where the text directly contradicted itself from one line to the next. And the matter of every noise text using a different working definition for noise was notable throughout. Further, as an aid to the combinatory process, indistinct subjects rather than specific nouns marked many of the quotations: the sentences were about "it" or "this" and the like. This allowed sentences with different topics to flow into each other and potentially create a partial coherence and sustained argument (even if contrary or unrelated to that of their original context). However, that vagary needed to be clarified or excised from the final text.

██████ As mentioned above, these contradictions did not, initially, bother me. The text was multivocal and indecisive just as the concept of noise is multivocal and undecidable. Had the experiment been simply designed to see what happens, that would have been enough. The result would have been fairly predictable: when you randomly collect 1,700 noise quotes, you get a randomly noisy text. But that would be much the same with randomly collected quotes on any topic or no topic at all or text randomly generated by algorithm. If writing were a random process, artificial intelligences would have overtaken the process long ago — only recently, through complex predictive algorithms, are they beginning to be used for writing the most basic reports. Something had to be done to clarify and contextualize the process, to shape and direct the textual noise just as I shaped and directed the sonic and visual noise of the *bruit jouissance* project into recognizable forms. The best metaphor for the writing process that I have is that my work was one of improvisation on and with noise over the indeterminate changes of the fragments on and of noise of the original text.

Noise is, however, marked by failure. The failure of the initial raw text to approach sufficient meaning or value as a philosophical argument (my desire to let the noise be noisy, forcing the reader to drown in disinformation overload with the vague hope that eventually they might surf its high tide) is not the failure of the project as a whole. The raw text and its juxtapositions do offer new lines of thought. There is value to the project. It just did not lie in leaving the work unedited or confusing by distracting digressions or individual associative connections. Moreover, this final text is not noise. It is noisy and it is a work of noise, but it is not noise. It has meaning, it makes sense, it makes and supports arguments. It does so in a noisy and nonstandard fashion, but in doing so it cannot be noise-as-such.

Another related question, then, might be: Did the experiment work?

The arguments on which I chose to focus this text are what I consider the formative positions of thorybology. And, in editing the text down, this text became much more of an argument for — or even a manifesto of — thorybology as a distinct noise theory/practice. These arguments include: being-as-noise, noise only being thinkable as ~~noise~~, the interruptive potential of noise, the need to use the creative and constructive potentials of noise against the oppressive and limiting potentials of noise, the possibility of reimagining the human relationship to the planet and the Anthropocene by a rethinking of our being-as-noise, and the possibility of that reimagining being used to limit the present climate crises. These theses weave their way in and out of the ( )holes and ruptures in the text, fading away only to be brought back, restated, clarified, fragmented, and retooled. And even with my additions and clarifications, they remained noisy.

████   But do they work? Do the arguments presented in this text offer those hoped for means of rethinking being-as-noise to reimagine coexistence? I argue that they do.

████   This work, for its normative force, draws heavily from the ecological work of Timothy Morton. Morton argues for an ecological thought, a method and process of thinking and reimagining human action and existence in the Anthropocene. The contention of this text is that noise and thorybology are alternate means of articulating that ecological thought. Thorybology contends that the confrontation with our disastrous and disruptive being-as-noise might force a change to a creative and open being-as-noise. Only by facing up to the enormity of the Anthropocene, only by acknowledging the human role in climate change, in the sixth mass extinction, can we act to mitigate and (if at all possible) reverse the consequences. This acknowledgement, I contend, involves the recognition that, as a human species, we have never existed in some idealized or idyllic state of nature. Since before dispersing from the African continent, humanity has been a disruptive and invasive species and now that we are aware and able to be aware of the situation, we must address it. Given that being-as-noise can be traced to the first human migrations and the resulting megafauna extinctions and the restructuring and engineering of the planet that can be traced to the earliest forms of agriculture and domestication, being-as-noise is not merely an industrial or postindustrial phenomena. Thus there is no point in the past to aspire to, no level of technology that is appropriate and beyond which is noise. This isn't to say that we aren't more disruptive now, that humanity hasn't caused more change in the last few centuries than in all previous millennia. But rather, I argue, these are changes in degree, not in kind. We have always been noisy. Noise, I contend, is one means of articulating and expressing the attributes that differentiate us as a species, that make us adaptable and inventive, and thus that make us disruptive and dangerous. If that is the case, then the solution is not to silence ourselves (which would likely result in just silencing the disenfranchised, the powerful being able to find exemptions for their noise), but rather to find better ways of being-as-noise, better ways of imagining our being-as-noise. My experiment sketches a possible program for thorybology, a program that can and should be expanded and further developed so that the change it advocates can come to pass.

So back to the success or failure of the experiment. The experiment is both a success and a failure. While noisy, it is not noise and the only noise that is properly considered within the text is ~~noise~~. That was an expected and inevitable failure. Further, it could not be left unedited without some authorial guidance on my part and still be considered a dissertation and that was the original purpose of this text. In order to succeed as a dissertation and as a monograph, the project had to fail to be noise. The raw text functioned as a beginning, as the means to generate novel juxtapositions that would indicate new lines of thought. It was incumbent upon me to follow those lines of thought forward. Randomization could not be counted upon to do that for me. However, the experiment worked. A text was generated, new lines of thought were explored, noise was researched and the resulting research remains, to a degree, noisy. As to the method's efficacy with other concepts, that is a test that demands another experiment. And as to its success in inducing political change, we can only hope.

LIST OF REFERENCES

Adorno, Theodor W. *Aesthetic Theory.* Translated by Robert
    Hullot-Kenter. Minneapolis: University of Minnesota Press,
    1997.
███████ *Negative Dialectics.* Translated by E.B. Ashton. New
    York: Continuum, 1973.
Amerika, Mark. *remixthebook.* Minneapolis: University of
    Minnesota Press, 2011.
███████ *Meta/Data: A Digital Poetics.* Cambridge: MIT Press,
    2009.
Attali, Jacques. *Noise: The Political Economy of Music.* Translat-
    ed by Brian Massumi. Minneapolis: University of Minnesota
    Press, 1985.
Badiou, Alain. *In Praise of Love.* Translated by Peter Bush. New
    York: New Press, 2012.
███████ *Philosophy for Militants.* Translated by Bruno Bosteels.
    New York: Verso, 2012.
Balestrini, Nanni. *Tristano #10546.* Translated by Mike Harakis.
    New York: Verso, 2014.
Ballard, J.G. *The Drowned World: A Novel.* New York: Liveright
    Publishing, 2012.
Barthes, Roland. *Image/Music/Text.* Translated by Stephen
    Heath. New York: Hill and Wang, 1977.

██████ *Roland Barthes.* Translated by Richard Howard. New York: Hill and Wang, 2010.

██████ *The Rustle of Language.* Translated by Richard Howard. Berkeley: University of California Press. 1989.

Bataille, Georges. *The Accursed Share: An Essay on General Economy, Vol. I: Consumption.* Translated by Robert Hurley. New York: Zone Books, 1991.

██████ *The Accursed Share, Vols. II & III: The History of Eroticism and Sovereignty.* Translated by Robert Hurley. New York: Zone Books, 1993.

██████ *Erotism: Death & Sensuality.* Translated by Mary Dalwood. San Francisco: City Lights Books, 1986.

██████ *Inner Experience.* Translated by Stuart Kendall. Albany: State University of New York Press, 2014.

██████ *Theory of Religion.* Translated by Robert Hurley. New York: Zone Books, 1992.

██████ *Visions of Excess: Selected Writings, 1927–1939.* Translated by Allan Stoekl. Minneapolis: University of Minnesota Press, 1985.

Bateman, Chris. *Chaos Ethics.* Winchester: Zero Books, 2014.

Baudrillard, Jean. *The Agony of Power.* Translated by Ames Hodges. Los Angeles: Semiotext(e), 2010.

██████ *Impossible Exchange.* Translated by Chris Turner. New York: Verso, 2011.

██████ *Passwords.* Translated by Chris Turner. New York: Verso, 2003.

██████ *Simulacra and Simulation.* Trans Shelia Faria Glaser. Ann Arbor: University of Michigan Press, 1994.

Benjamin, Walter. *The Arcades Project.* Edited by Hannah Arendt. Translated by Howard Eiland and Kevin McLaughlin. Cambridge: Harvard University Press, 2002.

██████ *Illuminations: Essays and Reflections.* Translated by Harry Zohn. New York: Schocken Books, 2007.

██████ *The Origin of German Tragic Drama.* Translated by John Osborne. New York: Verso, 2009.

███████ *Radio Benjamin*. Translated by Jonathan Lutes, Lisa Harries Schumann, and Diana K. Reese. New York: Verso, 2014.

Bentham, Jeremy. *The Panopticon Writings*. New York: Verso, 1995.

Berardi, Franco "Bifo." *Heroes: Mass Murder and Suicide*. New York: Verso, 2015.

Berg, Aase. *Dark Matter*. Translated by Johannes Göransson. Boston: Black Ocean, 2013.

Bök, Christian. *'Pataphysics: The Poetics of an Imaginary Science*. Evanston: Northwestern University Press, 2002.

Bray, Mark. *Translating Anarchy: The Anarchism of Occupy Wall Street*. Winchester: Zero Books, 2013.

Brecht, Bertolt. *Brecht on Theater: The Development of an Aesthetic*. Translated by John Willett. New York: Hill and Wang, 1992.

Brown, David P. *Noise Orders: Jazz, Improvisation, and Architecture*. Minneapolis: University of Minnesota Press, 2006.

Bryant, Levi R. *The Democracy of Objects*. Ann Arbor: Open Humanities Press, 2011.

███████ *Onto-Cartography: An Ontology of Machines and Media*. Edinburgh: Edinburgh University Press, 2014.

Bull, Malcolm. *Anti-Nietzsche*. New York: Verso, 2011.

Burkhardt, Andreas. *A Sanctuary of Sounds*. Brooklyn: punctum books, 2013.

Burroughs, William S. *The Soft Machine*. London: Fourth Estate, 2010.

███████ *Word Virus: The William Burroughs Reader*. Edited by James Grauerholz and Ira Silverberg. New York: Grove Press, 1998.

Cage, John. *Anarchy: New York City – January 1988*. Middletown: Wesleyan University Press, 2001.

███████ *Composition in Retrospect*. Cambridge: Exact Change, 1993.

███████ *Diary: How to Improve the World (You Will Only Make Matters Worse)*. Edited by Richard Kraft and Joe Biel. Los Angeles: Siglio Press, 2015.

███████ *Empty Words: Writings '73–'78.* Middletown: Wesleyan University Press, 1981.

███████ *M: Writings '67–'72.* Middletown: Wesleyan University Press, 1973.

███████ *Silence.* 50th Anniversary Edition. Middletown: Wesleyan University Press, 2011.

███████ *X: Writings '79–'82.* Middletown: Wesleyan University Press, 1983.

███████ *A Year From Monday: New Lectures and Writings.* Middletown: Wesleyan University Press, 1967.

Carroll, Peter J. *Liber Null and Psychonaut: An Introduction to Chaos Magic.* San Francisco: Weiser Books, 1987.

Chamayou, Grégorie. *A Theory of the Drone.* Translated by Janet Lloyd. New York: The New Press, 2013.

Cioran, E.M. *All Gall is Divided: The Aphorisms of a Legendary Iconoclast.* Translated by Richard Howard. New York: Arcade Publishing, 2012.

███████ *Drawn and Quartered.* Translated by Richard Howard. New York: Arcade Publishing, 2012.

Clemens, Justin, and Helen Johnson. *Black River.* Melbourne: re.press, 2007.

Cohen, Jeffrey Jerome (ed.). *Prismatic Ecology: Ecotheory Beyond Green.* Minneapolis: University of Minnesota Press, 2013.

Colebrook, Claire. *Death of the PostHuman: Essays on Extinction, Vol. 1.* Ann Arbor: Open Humanities Press, 2014.

Connole, Edia, Paul J. Ennis, and Nicola Masciandaro (eds.). *True Detection.* Schism Press², 2014.

Connolly, William E. *The Fragility of Things: Self-Organizing Processes, Neoliberal Fantasies, and Democratic Activism.* Durham: Duke University Press, 2013.

Critchley, Simon. *Infinitely Demanding: Ethics of Commitment, Politics of Resistance.* New York: Verso, 2012.

Daniel, Drew. *20 Jazz Funk Greats.* 33 1/3 series. New York: Bloomsbury, 2013.

Daumal, René. *Mount Analogue.* Translated by Carol Cosman. New York: Tusk Ivories, 2004.

███████ *Pataphysical Essays.* Translated by Thomas Vosteen. Cambridge: Wakefield Press, 2012.

Davis, Colin. "Hauntology, Spectres and Phantoms." *French Studies* 59, no. 3 (2005): 373–79. DOI: 10.1093/fs/kni143.

De Vos, Jan. "The Academy of Everyday Life: Psychology, Hauntology, and Psychoanalysis." *Educational Insights* 13, no. 4 (2009): 1–17.

Debord, Guy. *Comments on the Society of the Spectacle.* Translated by Malcolm Imrie. New York: Verso, 2011.

███████ *Society of the Spectacle.* Detroit: Black & Red, 1983.

Deleuze, Gilles. *Difference & Repetition.* Translated by Paul Patton. New York: Columbia University Press, 1994.

███████ *The Fold: Leibniz and the Baroque.* Translated by Tom Conley. Minneapolis: University of Minnesota Press, 1993.

███████ *Foucault.* Translated by Seán Hand. Minneapolis: University of Minnesota Press, 1986.

███████ *The Logic of Sense.* Translated by Mark Lester with Charles Stivale. New York: Columbia University Press, 1990.

Deleuze, Gilles, and Félix Guattari. *Anti-Oedipus: Capitalism and Schizophrenia.* Translated by Robert Hurley, Mark Seem, and Helen R. Lane. Minneapolis: University of Minnesota Press, 1983.

███████ *Kafka: Toward a Minor Literature.* Translated by Dana Polan. Minneapolis: University of Minnesota Press, 1986.

███████ *A Thousand Plateaus: Capitalism and Schizophrenia.* Translated by Brian Massumi. Minneapolis: University of Minnesota Press, 1987.

███████ *What Is Philosophy?* Translated by Hugh Tomlinson and Graham Burchell. New York: Columbia University Press, 1994.

DeLillo, Don. *White Noise.* London: Picador, 2012.

Demers, Joanna. *Listening through the Noise: The Aesthetics of Experimental Electronic Music.* New York: Oxford University Press, 2010.

Derrida, Jacques. *Acts of Religion.* Edited by Gil Anidjar. New York: Routledge, 2010.

█████ *The Animal That Therefore I Am.* Edited by Marie-Louis Mallet. Translated by David Willis. New York: Fordham University Press, 2008.

█████ *Aporias.* Translated by Thomas Dutoit. Stanford: Stanford University Press, 1993.

█████ *Archeology of the Frivolous: Reading Condillac.* Translated by John P. Leavey, Jr. Lincoln: University of Nebraska Press, 1980.

█████ *Cinders.* Translated by Ned Lukacher. Minneapolis: University of Minnesota Press, 2014. Print

█████ *Dissemination.* Translated by Barbara Johnson. New York: Continuum, 2004.

█████ *The Ear of the Other: Otobiography, Transference, Translation.* Edited by Christie McDonald. Translated by Peggy Kamuf and Avital Ronell. Lincoln: University of Nebraska Press, 1988.

█████ *Geneses, Genealogies, Genres, & Genius: The Secrets of the Archive.* Translated by Beverley Bie Brahic. New York: Columbia University Press, 2006.

█████ *Glas.* Translated by John P. Leavey, Jr. and Richard Rand. Lincoln: University of Nebraska Press, 1986.

█████ *Limited Inc.* Translated by Samuel Weber and Jeffrey Mehlman. Evanston: Northwestern University Press, 1988.

█████ *Margins of Philosophy.* Translated by Alan Bass. Chicago: University of Chicago Press, 1984.

█████ *Of Hospitality.* Translated by Rachel Bowlby. Stanford, California: Stanford University Press, 2000.

█████ *Of Spirit: Heidegger and the Question.* Translated by Geoffrey Bennington and Rachel Bowlby. Chicago: University of Chicago Press, 1989.

█████ *On Cosmopolitanism and Forgiveness.* Translated by Mark Dooley and Michael Hughes. New York: Routledge, 2001.

█████ *On the Name.* Translated by David Wood, John P. Leavey, Jr., and Ian McLeod. Stanford, California: Stanford University Press, 1995.

████ *The Politics of Friendship.* Translated by George Collins. New York: Verso, 2005.

████ *The Post Card: From Socrates to Freud and Beyond.* Translated by Alan Bass. Chicago: University of Chicago Press, 1987.

████ *Signéponge/Signsponge.* Translated by Richard Rand. New York: Columbia University Press, 1984.

████ *Sovereignties in Question: The Poetics of Paul Celan.* Edited by Thomas Dutoit and Outi Pasanen. New York: Fordham University Press, 2005.

████ *Specters of Marx: The State of the Debt, the Work of Mourning and the New International.* Translated by Peggy Kamuf. New York: Routledge, 2006.

████ *Spurs: Nietzsche's Styles.* Translated by Barbara Harlow. Chicago: University of Chicago Press, 1979.

████ *The Truth in Painting.* Translated by Geoff Bennington and Ian McLeod. Chicago: University of Chicago Press, 1987.

████ *Voice and Phenomenon: Introduction to the Problem of the Sign in Husserl's Phenomenology.* Translated by Leonard Lawlor. Evanston: Northwestern University Press, 2011.

████ *Who's Afraid of Philosophy? Right To Philosophy I.* Translated by Jan Plug. Stanford: Stanford University Press, 2002.

████ *Writing and Difference.* Translated by Alan Bass. Chicago: University of Chicago Press, 1978.

Derrida, Jacques, and Bernard Stiegler. *Echographies of Television.* Translated by Jennifer Bajorek. Cambridge: Polity, 2002.

Doyle, Sir Arthur Conan. *The Complete Professor Challenger Stories.* London: Wordsworth Editions, 1989.

Dyson, Frances. *Sounding New Media: Immersion and Embodiment in the Arts and Culture.* Berkeley: University of California Press, 2009.

████ *The Tone of Our Times: Sound, Sense, Economy, and Ecology.* Cambridge: MIT Press, 2014.

Epstein, Josh. *Sublime Noise: Musical Culture and the Modernist Writer.* Baltimore: Johns Hopkins University Press, 2014.

Flusser, Vilém. *Natural:Mind*. Translated by Rodrigo Maltez Novaes. Minneapolis: Univocal, 2013.

Foucault, Michel. *The Archaeology of Knowledge & the Discourse on Language*. Translated by A.M. Sheridan Smith. New York: Pantheon Books, 1972.

Freud, Sigmund. *Moses and Monotheism*. Translated by Katherine Jones. New York: Vintage Books, 1967.

Galloway, Alexander. *Laruelle: Against the Digital*. Minneapolis: University of Minnesota Press, 2014.

Galloway, Alexander, Eugene Thacker, and McKenzie Wark. *Excommunication: Three Inquiries in Media and Mediation*. Chicago: University of Chicago Press, 2014.

Goddard, Michael, Benjamin Halligan, and Nicola Spelman (eds.). *Resonances: Noise and Contemporary Music*. New York: Bloomsbury, 2013.

Goddard, Michael, Bejamin Halligan, and Paul Hegarty (eds.). *Reverberations: The Philosophy, Aesthetics, and Politics of Noise*. New York: Continuum, 2012.

Goldsmith, Mike. *Discord: The Story of Noise*. Oxford: Oxford University Press, 2012.

Goodman, Steve. *Sonic Warfare: Sound, Affect, and the Ecology of Fear*. Cambridge: MIT Press, 2010.

Graeber, David. *Fragments of an Anarchist Anthropology*. Chicago: Prickly Paradigm Press, 2004.

Grimshaw, Jeremy. *Draw a Straight Line and Follow It: The Music and Mysticism of La Monte Young*. Oxford: Oxford University Press, 2011.

Guattari, Félix. *The Three Ecologies*. Translated by Ian Pindar and Paul Sutton. New York: Continuum, 2008.

Gunkel, David J., and Ted Gournelos (eds.). *Transgression 2.0: Media, Culture, and the Politics of a Digital Age*. New York: Continuum, 2012.

Hanh, Thich Nhat. *Silence: The Power of Quiet in a World Full of Noise*. New York: HarperOne, 2015.

███████ *The World We Have: A Buddhist Approach to Peace and Ecology*. Berkeley: Parallax Press, 2008.

Hall, Steven. *The Raw Shark Texts*. New York: Cannongate, 2007.

Hainge, Greg. *Noise Matters: Towards an Ontology of Noise*. New York: Bloomsbury, 2013.

Halberstam, Judith. *The Queer Art of Failure*. Durham: Duke University Press, 2011.

Harmon, Graham. *Bells and Whistles: More Speculative Realism*. Winchester: Zero Books, 2013.

██████ *Weird Realism: Lovecraft and Philosophy*. Washington: Zero Books, 2012.

Hayden, Ethan. *( )*. 33 1/3 series. New York: Bloomsbury, 2014.

Hayles, N. Katherine. *How We Think: Digital Media and Contemporary Technologies*. Chicago: University of Chicago Press, 2012.

Hearne, Kevin. *Star Wars: Heir to the Jedi*. New York: Del Rey, 2015.

Hegarty, Paul. *Noise/Music: A History*. New York: Bloomsbury, 2007.

██████ "Noise Threshold: Merzbow and the End of Natural Sound." *Organized Sound* 6, no. 3 (2001): 193–200. DOI: 10.1017/S1355771801003053.

Heller-Roazen, Daniel. *The Fifth Hammer: Pythagoras and the Disharmony of the World*. New York: Zone Books, 2011.

Hendy, David. Noise: *A Human History of Sound and Listening*. London: ECCO, 2013.

Holmes, Jamie. *Nonsense: The Power of Not Knowing*. New York: Crown Publishers, 2015.

Horkheimer, Max, and Theodor W. Adorno. *Dialectic of Enlightenment*. Translated by John Cumming. New York: Continuum, 1996.

Hughes, Chris. "Dialogue Between Fukuyama's Account of the End of History and Derrida's Hauntology." *Journal of Philosophy: A Cross-Disciplinary Inquiry* 7, no. 18 (2012): 13–26. DOI: 10.5840/jphilnepal201271813

Hugill, Andrew. *'Pataphysics: A Useless Guide*. Cambridge: MIT Press, 2012.

Ikoniadou, Eleni. *The Rhythmic Event: Art, Media, and the Sonic.* Cambridge: MIT Press, 2014.

The Invisible Committee. *To Our Friends.* Translated by Robert Hurley. South Pasadena: Semiotext(e), 2015.

Joseph, Branden W. *Beyond the Dream Syndicate: Tony Conrad and the Arts after Cage.* New York: Zone Books, 2011.

Kahn, Douglas. *Earth Sound Earth Signal: Energies and Earth Magnitude in the Arts.* Berkeley: University of California Press, 2013.

██████ *Noise Water Meat: A History of Sound in the Arts.* Cambridge: MIT Press, 1999.

Kant, Immanuel. *Perpetual Peace and Other Essays.* Translated by Ted Humphrey. Indianapolis: Hackett Publishing Company, 1983.

Keizer, Garret. *The Unwanted Sound of Everything We Want: A Book About Noise.* New York: PublicAffairs, 2010.

Keller, Ed, Nicola Masciandaro, and Eugene Thacker (eds.). *Leper Creativity: Cyclonopedia Symposium.* Brooklyn: punctum books, 2012.

Kelly, Caleb. *Cracked Media: The Sound of Malfunction.* Cambridge: MIT Press, 2009.

Kierkegaard, Søren. *The Concept of Anxiety: A Simple Psychologically Orienting Deliberation on the Dogmatic Issue of Hereditary Sin.* Translated by Reidar Thomte. Princeton, New Jersey: Princeton University Press, 1980.

Kolbert, Elizabeth. *The Sixth Extinction: An Unnatural History.* New York: Picador, 2014.

Koolhaas, Rem. *Delirious New York: A Retroactive Manifesto for Manhattan.* New York: The Monacelli Press, 1994.

Kosko, Bart. *Noise.* New York: Viking, 2006

Krapp, Peter. *Noise Channels: Glitch and Error in Digital Culture.* Minneapolis: University of Minnesota Press, 2011.

Kristeva, Julia. *Powers of Horror: An Essay on Abjection.* Translated by Leon S. Roudiez. New York: Columbia University Press, 1982.

LaBelle, Brandon. *Background Noise: Perspectives on Sound Art.* New York: Continuum, 2006.

Lacan, Jacques. *On the Names-of-the-Father.* Translated by
Bruce Fink. Malden: Polity Press, 2013.

Land, Nick. *Fanged Noumena: Collected Writings 1987–2007.*
Falmouth: Urbanomic, 2011.

███ *The Thirst for Annihilation: Georges Bataille and Viru-
lent Nihilism.* New York: Routledge, 1992.

Lao-Tzu. *Lao-Tzu: Te-Tao Ching: A New Translation Based on
the Recently Discovered Ma-wang-tui Texts.* Translated by
Robert G. Henricks. New York: Ballantine Books, 1989.

Latour, Bruno. *Politics of Nature: How to Bring the Sciences into
Democracy.* Translated by Catherine Porter. Cambridge:
Harvard University Press, 2004.

███ *Reassembling the Social: An Introduction to Actor-Net-
work-Theory.* New York: Oxford University Press, 2007.

███ *We Have Never Been Modern.* Translated by Catherine
Porter. Cambridge: Harvard University Press, 1993.

Laruelle, François. *From Decision To Heresy: Experiments in
Non-Standard Thought.* Edited by Robin Mackay. New York:
Sequence Press, 2012.

███ *Future Christ: A Lesson in Heresy.* Translated by Anthony Paul Smith. New York: Continuum, 2010.

███ *Struggle and Utopia at the End Times of Philosophy.*
Translated by Drew S. Burk and Anthony Paul Smith. Minneapolis: Univocal, 2012.

Lazzarato, Maurizio. *Governing by Debt.* Translated by Joshua
David Jordan. South Pasadena: Semiotext(e), 2015.

Lefebvre, Henri. *Rhythmalaysis: Space, Time and Everyday Life.*
Translated by Stuart Elden and Gerald Moore. New York:
Bloomsbury, 2013.

Ligotti, Thomas. *The Conspiracy Against The Human Race: A
Contrivance of Horror.* New York: Hippocampus Press, 2010.

Lotringer, Sylvère. *Mad Like Artaud.* Translated by Joanna
Spinks. Minneapolis: Univocal, 2015.

Lovecraft, H.P. *The Call of Cthulhu and Other Weird Stories.*
Edited by S.T. Joshi. New York: Penguin Books, 1999.

Lovink, Geert. *Networks without a Cause: A Critique of Social
Media.* Malden: Polity, 2011.

Lucier, Alvin. *Music 109: Notes on Experimental Music.* Middletown: Wesleyan University Press, 2012.

Luke, Megan R. *Kurt Schwitters: Space, Image, Exile.* Chicago: University of Chicago Press, 2014.

M. *Un-Sight/ Un-Sound (delirium X.).* New York: gnOme books, 2014.

Mackay, Robin (ed.). *Collapse: Philosophical Research and Development.* Volume II. 2007; rpt. Falmouth: Urbanomic, 2012.

███████ *Collapse: Philosophical Research and Development.* Volume III. 2007; rpt. Falmouth: Urbanomic, 2012.

███████ *Collapse: Philosophical Research and Development.* Volume IV. 2008; rpt. Falmouth: Urbanomic, 2012.

Mackay, Robin, and Armen Avanessian (eds.). *#Accelerate: The Accelerationist Reader.* Falmouth: Urbanomic, 2014.

Masciandaro, Nicola (ed.). *Hideous Gnosis: Black Metal Theory Symposium I.* CreateSpace, 2010.

Maciandaro, Nicola, and Eugene Thacker (eds.). *Glossator: Practice and Theory of the Commentary 7*, issue titled "The Mystical Text (Black Clouds Course through Me Unending …)" (2013).

Maeterlinck, Maurice. *The Life of the Bee.* Translated by Alfred Sutro. New York: Dodd, Mead and Co., 1964.

Meeks, Wayne A. "Jeremiah." *The HarperCollins Study Bible New Revised Standard Version.* New York: HarperCollins, 1993.

Meillassoux, Quentin. *After Finitude: An Essay on the Necessity of Contingency.* Translated by Ray Brassier. New York: Continuum, 2008.

███████ *The Number and the Siren: A Decipherment of Mallarmé's* Coup De Dés. New York: Sequence Press, 2011.

███████ *Science Fiction and Extro-Science Fiction.* Translated by Alyosh Edlebi. Minneapolis: Univocal, 2015.

Meyer, Leonard B. *Music, the Arts, and Ideas: Patters and Predictions in Twentieth-Century Culture.* Chicago: University of Chicago Press, 1994.

Miller, Paul D. (ed.). *Sound Unbound: Sampling Digital Music and Culture*. Cambridge: MIT Press, 2008.

Mills, Jon. "Lacan on Paranoiac Knowledge." *Psychoanalytic Psychology* 20, no. 1 (2003): 30–51. DOI: 10.1037/0736-9735.20.1.30.

Minter, Adam. *Junkyard Planet: Travels in the Billion-Dollar Trash Trade*. New York: Bloomsbury, 2013.

Mitchell, Andrew J., and Sam Slote (eds.). *Derrida and Joyce: Texts and Contexts*. Albany: State University of New York Press, 2013.

Morris, Joe. *Perpetual Frontier: The Properties of Free Music*. Stony Creek: Riti Publishing, 2012.

Morton, Timothy. *Dark Ecology: For a Logic of Future Coexistence*. New York: Columbia University Press, 2016.

███ *The Ecological Thought*. Cambridge: Harvard University Press, 2010.

███ *Ecology Without Nature: Rethinking Environmental Aesthetics*. Cambridge: Harvard University Press, 2007.

███ *Hyperobjects: Philosophy and Ecology after the End of the World*. Minneapolis: University of Minnesota Press, 2013.

███ *Realist Magic: Objects, Ontology, Causality*. Ann Arbor: Open Humanities Press, 2013.

Moss, Donald. *Thirteen Ways of Looking at a Man: Psychoanalysis and Masculinity*. New York: Routledge, 2012.

Nancy, Jean-Luc. *After Fukushima: The Equivalence of Catastrophes*. Translated by Charlotte Mandell. New York: Fordham University Press, 2015.

███ *Listening*. Translated by Charlotte Mandell. New York: Fordham University Press, 2007.

Nechvatal, Joseph. *Immersion into Noise*. Ann Arbor: Open Humanities Press, 2011.

Negarestani, Reza. *Cyclonopedia: Complicity with Anonymous Materials*. Melbourne: re.press, 2008.

Nietzsche, Friedrich. *Basic Writings of Nietzsche*. Translated by Walter Kaufmann. New York: The Modern Library, 2000.

███████ *The Dionysian Vision of the World.* Translated by Ira J. Allen. Minneapolis: Univocal, 2013.

███████ *Human, All Too Human: A Book For Free Spirits.* Translated by R.J. Hollingdale. New York: Cambridge University Press, 1996.

███████ *Thus Spoke Zarathustra.* Translated by Graham Parkes. Oxford: Oxford University Press, 2005.

███████ *Writings from the Early Notebooks.* Edited by Raymond Geuss and Alexander Nehamas. Translated by Ladislaus Löb. Cambridge: Cambridge University Press, 2010.

Nunes, Mark (ed.). *Error: Glitch, Noise, and Jam in New Media Cultures.* New York: Bloomsbury, 2011.

Orr, Jackie. *Panic Diaries: A Genealogy of Panic Disorder.* Durham: Duke University Press, 2006.

Panzner, Joe. *The Process That Is The World: Cage/Deleuze/Events/Performances.* New York: Bloomsbury, 2015.

Poe, Edgar Allan. *The Raven: Tales and Poems.* New York: Penguin Books, 2013.

Priest, eldritch. *Boring Formless Nonsense: Experimental Music and the Aesthetics of Failure.* New York: Bloomsbury, 2013.

Prigogine, Ilya. *The End of Certainty: Time, Chaos, and the New Laws of Nature.* New York: The Free Press, 1997.

Prochnik, George. *In Pursuit of Silence: Listening for Meaning in a World of Noise.* New York: Doubleday, 2010.

Rancière, Jacques. *Hatred of Democracy.* Translated by Steve Corcoran. New York: Verso, 2014.

███████ *The Intervals of Cinema.* Translated by John Howe. New York: Verso, 2014.

███████ *On the Shores of Politics.* Translated by Liz Heron. New York: Verso, 2007.

Raskin, Jimmy. *The Prologue, The Poltergeist, and the Hollow Tree: Recalling the Tightrope Walker from* Thus Spoke Zarathustra. New York: Nyehaus/Foundation 20 21, 2005.

Raunig, Gerald. *A Thousand Machines: A Concise Philosophy of the Machine as Social Movement.* Trans Aileen Derieg. Los Angeles: Semiotext(e), 2010.

Ray, Robert B. *How a Film Theory God Lost and Other Mysteries in Cultural Studies.* Bloomington: Indiana University Press, 2001.

Rigby, Kate. *Dancing With Disaster: Environmental Histories, Narratives, and Ethics for Perilous Times.* Charlottesville: University of Virginia Press, 2015.

Ross, Alex. *The Rest Is Noise: Listening to the Twentieth Century.* New York: Picador, 2012.

Rothstein, Adam. *Drone.* New York: Bloomsbury, 2015.

Russolo, Luigi, and Francesco Balilla Pratella. *The Art of Noise: Destruction of Music by Futurist Machines.* Edited by Candice Black. London: Sun Vision Press, 2012.

Sampson, Tony D. *Virality: Contagion Theory in The Age of Networks.* Minneapolis: University of Minnesota Press, 2012.

Schafer, R. Murray. *The Soundscape: Our Sonic Environment and the Tuning of the World.* Rochester: Destiny Books, 1994.

Schneider, Eric D., and Dorion Sagan. *Into The Cool: Energy Flow, Thermodynamics, and Life.* Chicago: University of Chicago Press, 2005.

Schopenhauer, Arthur. *The World as Will and Representation, Volume 1.* Translated by E.F.J. Payne. New York: Dover, 1969.

Schwartz, Hillel. *Making Noise: From Babel to the Big Bang & Beyond.* New York: Zone Books, 2011.

Schwitters, Kurt. *Lucky Hans: And Other Merz Fairy Tales.* Princeton: Princeton University Press, 2009.

Scranton, Roy. *Learning to Die in the Anthropocene: Reflections on the End of a Civilization.* San Francisco: City Lights Books, 2015.

Serres, Michel. *Biogea.* Translated by Randolph Burks. Minneapolis: Univocal, 2012. Print

▬▬▬ *The Five Senses: A Philosophy of Mingled Bodies.* Translated by Margaret Sankey and Peter Cowley. New York: Continuum, 2008.

▬▬▬ *Genesis.* Translated by Geneviève James and James Nielson. Ann Arbor: University of Michigan Press, 1995.

■■■■■■ *Malfeasance: Appropriation Through Pollution?* Translated by Anne-Marie Feenberg-Dibon. Stanford: Stanford University Press, 2011.

■■■■■■ *The Natural Contract.* Translated by Elizabeth MacArthur and William Paulson. Ann Arbor: University of Michigan Press, 2011.

■■■■■■ *The Parasite.* Translated by Lawrence R. Schehr. Minneapolis: University of Minnesota Press, 2007.

■■■■■■ *Times of Crisis: What the Financial Crisis Revealed and How to Reinvent Our Lives and Future.* Translated by Anne-Marie Feenberg-Dibon. New York: Bloomsbury, 2014.

■■■■■■ *The Troubadour of Knowledge.* Translated by Sheila Faria Glaser with William Paulson. Ann Arbor: University of Michigan Press, 1997.

Serres, Michel, with Bruno Latour. *Conversations on Science, Culture, and Time.* Translated by Roxanne Lapidus. Ann Arbor: The University of Michigan Press, 1998.

Shannon, Claude E., and Warren Weaver. *The Mathematical Theory of Communication.* Chicago: University of Illinois Press, 1998.

Sim, Stuart. *Manifesto for Silence: Confronting the Politics and Culture of Noise.* Edinburgh: Edinburgh University Press, 2004.

Simondon, Gilbert. *Two Lessons on Man and Animal.* Translated by Drew S. Burk. Minneapolis: Univocal, 2012.

Sloterdijk, Peter. *Nietzsche Apostle.* Translated by Steven Corcoran. Los Angeles: Semiotext(e), 2013.

Sterne, Jonathan. *MP3: The Meaning of a Format.* Durham: Duke University Press, 2012.

Stewart, John, with Arline L. Bronzaft, Francis McManus, Nigel Rodgers, and Val Weedon. *Why Noise Matters: A Worldwide Perspective on the Problems, Policies and Solutions.* New York: Earthscan, 2011.

Stiegler, Bernard. *Symbolic Misery, Volume 1: The Hyperindustrial Epoch.* Malden: Polity Press, 2014.

Suzuki, D.T. *An Introduction to Zen Buddhism.* New York: Grove Press, 1964.

Thacker, Eugene. *Cosmic Pessimism.* Minneapolis: Univocal, 2015.
██████ *An Ideal For Living.* Schism Press², 2014.
██████ *In the Dust of This Planet: Horror of Philosophy, Vol. 1.* Winchester: Zero Books, 2011.
██████ *Starry Speculative Corpse: Horror of Philosophy, Vol. 2.* Winchester: Zero Books, 2015.
██████ *Tentacles Longer Than Night: Horror of Philosophy, Volume 3.* Winchester: Zero Books, 2015.
Thompson, Hunter S. *Fear and Loathing in Las Vegas: A Savage Journey to the Heart of the American Dream.* New York: Vintage Books, 1998.
Toop, David. *Sinister Resonance: The Mediumship of the Listener.* New York: Continuum, 2010.
Trigg, Dylan. *The Thing: A Phenomenology of Horror.* Winchester: Zero Books, 2014.
Tugen, Rasu-Yong, *Baroness De Tristeombre: Songs from the Black Moon.* New York: gnOme books, 2014.
Ulmer, Gregory L. *Avatar Emergency.* Anderson: Parlor Press, 2012.
██████ *Electracy: Gregory L. Ulmer's Textshop Experiments.* Edited by Craig J. Saper, Gregory L. Ulmer, and Victor J. Vitanza. Middletown: The Davies Group, 2015.
██████ *Heuretics: The Logic of Invention.* Baltimore: Johns Hopkins University Press, 1994.
██████ *Internet Invention: From Literacy to Electracy.* New York: Longman, 2003.
Van der Braak, André. *Nietzsche and Zen: Self-Overcoming Without a Self.* New York: Lexington Books, 2011.
Virilio, Paul. *Negative Horizon: An Essay in Dromoscopy.* New York: Continuum, 2008.
Viveiros de Castro, Eduardo. *Cannibal Metaphysics: For A Post-Structural Anthropology.* Translated by Peter Skafish. Minneapolis: Univocal, 2014.
Voegelin, Salomé. *Sonic Possible Worlds: Hearing the Continuum of Sound.* New York: Bloomsbury, 2014.
Volcler, Juliette. *Extremely Loud: Sound as a Weapon.* Translated by Carol Volk. New York: The New Press, 2013.

Wark, McKenzie. *Molecular Red: Theory for the Anthropocene.* New York: Verso, 2015.

██████ *The Spectacle of Disintegration: Situationist Passages Out of the 20th Century.* New York: Verso, 2013.

██████ *Telesthesia: Communication, Culture & Class.* Malden: Polity, 2012.

Warner, Brad. *Hardcore Zen: Punk Rock, Monster Movies, & the Truth About Reality.* Boston: Wisdom Publications, 2003.

Watson, Ben. *Derek Bailey and the Story of Free Improvisation.* New York: Verso, 2013.

Whitman, Walt. *Leaves of Grass.* 150th Anniversary Edition. The First (1855) Edition. New York: Penguin Books, 2005.

Williams, Evan Calder. *Combined and Uneven Apocalypse.* Winchester: Zero Books, 2010.

Wilson, Robert Anton. *Cosmic Trigger Volume I: Final Secret of the Illuminati.* Tempe: New Falcon Publications, 1977.

██████ *Right Where You Are Sitting Now: Further Tales of the Illuminati.* Oakland: Ronin, 1992.

Wilson, Scott (ed.). *Melancology: Black Metal Theory and Ecology.* Winchester: Zero Books, 2014.

Wittgenstein, Ludwig. *Tractatus Logico-Philosophicus.* Translated by C.K. Ogden. New York: Barnes & Noble, 2003.

Woodward, Brett. *Merzbook: The Plesuredome of Noise.* Melbourne: Extreme, 1999.

Young, Rob (ed.). *Undercurrents: The Hiding Wiring of Modern Music.* New York: Continuum, 2002.

Zalamea, Fernando. *Synthetic Philosophy of Contemporary Mathematics.* Translated by Zachary Luke Fraser. New York: Sequence Press, 2012.

Žižek, Slavoj. *For They Know Not What They Do: Enjoyment as a Political Factor.* New York: Verso, 2008.

Zorn, John (ed.). *Arcana: Musicians on Music.* New York: Granary Books/Hips Road, 2000.

██████ *Arcana II: Musicians on Music.* New York: Hips Road/Tzadik, 2007.

██████ *Arcana III: Musicians on Music.* New York: Hips Road/Tzadik, 2008.

"W. dreams, like Phaedrus, of an army of thinker-friends, thinker-lovers. He dreams of a thought-army, a thought-pack, which would storm the philosophical Houses of Parliament. He dreams of Tartars from the philosophical steppes, of thought-barbarians, thought-outsiders. What distance would shine in their eyes!"

— Lars Iyer